100

THINGS TO DO IN
SAN ANTONIO
BEFORE YOU
DIE

100
THINGS TO DO IN
SAN ANTONIO
BEFORE YOU
DIE

2nd Edition

• •

DENISE BARKIS RICHTER, Ph.D.

REEDY PRESS

Copyright © 2019 by Reedy Press, LLC
Reedy Press
PO Box 5131
St. Louis, MO 63139, USA
www.reedypress.com

Library of Congress Control Number: 2018962604

ISBN: 9781681061993

Text and photos by Denise Barkis Richter, Ph.D.
Cover image: Shutterstock
Image on page ii: Aedan Richter
Back cover image: Pableaux Johnson

Design by Jill Halpin

Printed in the United States of America
19 20 21 22 23   5 4 3 2 1

Please note that websites, phone numbers, addresses, and company names are subject to change or cancellation. We did our best to relay the most accurate information available, but due to circumstances beyond our control, please do not hold us liable for misinformation. When exploring new destinations, please do your homework before you go.

DEDICATION

To my fellow San Antonio bloggers, my Readhead Book Group, the Professional Tour Guide Association of San Antonio, my teachers, my students, my colleagues, my friends, my mother and father, my siblings, my BFF Amy, and especially my husband and daughter, who let me photograph their food before they dig in.

• •

CONTENTS

• •

Food and Drink

Music and Entertainment

Sports and Recreation

• •

• •

PREFACE

I love to travel, and I love to write about traveling. Because my gallivanting budget is limited, I decided to become a tourist in my own town, San Antonio, Texas, which happens to be one of the most beautiful, historic, and romantic cities on the planet.

I've been writing about fun things to do and see in the Alamo City on my blog, sanantoniotourist.net, since 2010. (Please follow me on Facebook at facebook.com/SanAntonioTourist!) It makes me happy to receive comments from San Antonio natives who discover something new through my blog or from visitors who thank me for helping them plan a memorable visit to San Antonio.

I moved to San Antonio in 1979 as an eighteen-year-old freshman in college, and I have grown to love my adopted city. I hope that some of my *amor* for the Alamo City rubs off on you.

It is my sincerest wish that both visitors and natives will use this book as your passport to fun! Each time you experience one of the hundred things, write the day you did it in the margins along with who accompanied you and a favorite memory. This book will become a treasured keepsake.

¡Disfrute! (Enjoy!) ¡Viva San Antonio!

• •

CULTURE AND HISTORY

REMEMBER THE ALAMO

Once, while I was traveling through Ireland, my bus driver confessed that he played hooky every time John Wayne's 1960 movie *The Alamo* came on TV. Though the historic mission is tiny in person, its reputation is grand throughout the world. It's the number one travel destination in Texas, and it and San Antonio's four other eighteenth-century Spanish colonial missions are a UNESCO World Heritage Site, the only one in Texas and one of only twenty-three in the United States. On the Ireland trip, I happened to have a faux coonskin cap with me, and I gave it to the teary-eyed driver. Yes, the Alamo delivers that kind of emotional impact. Don't miss it.

300 Alamo Plaza
(210) 225-1391
thealamo.org

MEANDER ALONG
THE RIVER WALK

San Antonio's River Walk, also known as the Paseo del Rio, on the San Antonio River is one of the most beautiful spots in the United States. No brag, just fact. Ask anyone who's been. The day after Thanksgiving through the Feast of the Epiphany in early January has always been my favorite time of year in downtown San Antonio. Twinkling lights in the trees along the River Walk create a magical space that transports you into a different realm. Strolling along the Paseo del Rio in a sea of lights will put even the grinchiest of grinches in a good mood. Throughout the year, you will also enjoy experiencing the river being dyed green for St. Patrick's Day, the Fiesta River Parade, Spurs championship parades, arts and crafts fairs, restaurants, bars, clubs, and shopping, all thanks to architect Robert H. H. Hugman, whose 1929 proposal saved the river from being paved over and used as a storm sewer. Works Progress Administration funds post-Depression sealed the deal. Thank you, FDR.

(210) 227-4262
thesanantonioriverwalk.com

EXPLORE YOUR HERITAGE
AT THE INSTITUTE OF TEXAN CULTURES

The University of Texas at San Antonio's Institute of Texan Cultures celebrates the diverse ethnicities and settlement groups that have made Texas great: Belgian, Swiss, Filipino, Hungarian, Polish, Wendish, German, Irish, Jewish, Lebanese, Syrian, Anglo, Chinese, Dutch, English, French, Greek, Italian, Scottish, Czech, Japanese, Native American, Tejano, African-American, Danish, Norwegian, Swedish, Spanish, and Mexican. Hour-long guided tours of the ITC museum are available to the public along with an archive, library, and photo collection for family history research. For more than forty years, the institute has hosted its annual Texas Folklife Festival, the biggest cultural celebration in Texas. More than forty cultural groups celebrate their heritage through food, music, dance, arts, and crafts. It's one of San Antonio's best events. Put it on your bucket list! It will become an annual event for you, too.

801 E. César E. Chávez Blvd.
(210) 485-2300
texancultures.com

5

TAKE IN SAN ANTONIO'S
ART MUSEUMS AND GALLERIES

The Alamo City is blessed with an abundance of art museums and galleries. "Arte Es Vida" ("Art Is Life") is a bumper sticker you'll see around town. No need to travel to Los Angeles, New York City, London, Paris, or Rome. Chances are we have something by your favorite artist or from your favorite time period right here. If I had to pick just one art museum to visit while I was in town, I'd choose the McNay because I love the setting and the collection; however, being asked to select one museum is like being asked to pick your favorite child. It's too painful. I love them all for different reasons, so please visit all of them.

Artpace San Antonio
445 N. Main Ave.
(210) 212-4900
artpace.org

Blue Star Contemporary
116 Blue Star
(210) 227-6960
bluestarart.org

Briscoe Western Art Museum
210 W. Market St.
(210) 299-4499
briscoemuseum.org

Culture Commons Gallery
115 Plaza de Armas
(210) 206-2787
getcreativesanantonio.com/explore-san-antonio/
city-exhibits/culture-commons

McNay Art Museum
6000 N. New Braunfels Ave.
(210) 824-5368
mcnayart.org

San Antonio Museum of Art
200 W. Jones Ave.
(210) 978-8100
samuseum.org

Southwest School of Art Exhibition Galleries
300 Augusta St.
(210) 200-8200
swschool.org

BROWSE
THE ALAMO CITY'S PUBLIC LIBRARIES

For those of us with children who've watched the *Spy Kids* movies written and directed by San Antonio native Robert Rodriguez, you'll recognize San Antonio's Central Library in downtown San Antonio as the OSS headquarters in *SK2*. Designed by Mexican architect Ricardo Legorreta, the edifice is known for its enchilada-red exterior. Inside you'll find computers with free Internet connectivity; a comfortable place to cool off while you peruse magazines and books; an art gallery; a Dale Chihuly glass sculpture titled *Fiesta Tower*; a Fernando Botero horse sculpture; and a mural by esteemed San Antonio artist Jesse Treviño. San Antonio boasts twenty-six branch libraries scattered throughout the city in addition to the Central Library. Landa Branch Library, housed in a 1920s Mediterranean-style mansion at 233 Bushnell, is my favorite. Be sure to enjoy the Carlos Cortés-designed *faux bois* pavilion in the garden while you're there.

600 Soledad
(210) 207-2500
mysapl.org

GET YOUR SPOOK ON

Spirits of those who died during the Battle of the Alamo, hotel housekeepers who met an untimely end but are still driven to tidy up, and Captain Richard King, founder of the King Ranch, are all apparitions you might encounter while on a ghost tour of downtown San Antonio. Tales of La Llorona (The Weeping Woman), the Donkey Lady, and the haunted railroad tracks on the South Side abound, so sign up for a candlelight ghost tour with the Sisters Grimm while you're in town to see if you stumble upon the supernatural. The sisters, descendants of San Antonio's Canary Islands founders, weave tales of the city's history throughout the hour and a half walking tour that covers the Alamo, the Menger Hotel, the Emily Morgan Hotel, San Fernando Cathedral, the Bexar County Courthouse, the Spanish Governor's Palace, the O'Henry House Museum, and Casa Navarro over approximately 2.5 miles.

204 Alamo Plaza
(210) 638-1338
sistersgrimmghosttour.com

FEEL THE SPIRIT
AT HOLY REDEEMER CATHOLIC CHURCH

Those who think you can only find gospel music at Baptist churches haven't been to Holy Redeemer, a Catholic church on San Antonio's East Side. I started going to Holy Redeemer back in the 1980s whenever I needed a spirit boost. The choir, backed by an amazing band and organist, would come into the church singing "Hosanna, blessed be the rock of my salvation," and I could feel the energy. I once brought a friend who grew up in Sweden to Mass at Holy Redeemer, and she turned to me and thanked me halfway through the service. When a woman by the name of Mrs. Ferguson (since deceased) sang, goosebumps would spring up over my entire body. Mrs. Ferguson may be gone, but Holy Redeemer is in good hands. An all-girls choir performed at a recent 9 a.m. Sunday Mass. Holy Redeemer celebrated its one-hundredth birthday in 2013, and the historic original church now serves as the narthex of the new sanctuary. All are welcome.

1819 Nevada St.
(210) 532-5358
facebook.com/pages/Holy-Redeemer-Church/123860577662229

STROLL
THROUGH HISTORIC LA VILLITA

San Antonio's La Villita (little village) is the city's original melting pot. Native Americans, Mexicans, Spaniards, East Texans, Texas Rangers, Germans, Swiss, French, and Anglos all called this little piece of land home. Located in the shadow of the Hilton Palacio del Rio along the banks of the San Antonio River on South Alamo Street at Nueva Street, La Villita's melting pot heritage lives on today through the countless festivals that are held here each year: Night in Old San Antonio, Soul Food Festival, Diwali: Festival of Light, St. Patrick's Day Festival, Mardi Gras, Fiesta Noche del Rio, and the Diez y Seis de Septiembre Celebration, to name a few. If you aren't in town for one of these festivals, don't worry. The shops, galleries, restaurants, and Little Church of La Villita offer plenty to do and see.

418 Villita St.
(210) 207-8614
getcreativesanantonio.com/exploresanantonio/lavillita

IMAGINE LATE NINETEENTH-CENTURY LIFE
IN KING WILLIAM

Surely the spirit of Walter Nold Mathis still roams the dazzling rooms and lovely grounds of his beloved Villa Finale, a grand 1876 Italianate home in San Antonio's King William neighborhood, the first historic neighborhood in Texas. Even if Mathis's spirit doesn't ramble around, his essence definitely lingers on through his immense collection of fine and decorative arts. The Villa Finale is the first National Trust Historic Site in Texas, and Mathis left plenty behind for visitors to peruse: Napoleonic memorabilia, including a death mask of the French emperor; snuff and match boxes; letter openers; Greek and Russian religious items; sterling silver coffee and tea sets; pewter plates, mugs, and serving pieces; prints by the artist Mary Bonner; bronze statues; Italian paintings; more than two thousand books; English Wedgwood; and on and on. Villa Finale is a wonderful example of the magnificent homes in this historic neighborhood built by German immigrants. Both Villa Finale and the Edward Steves Homestead are open for public tours.

ourkwa.org
villafinale.org
saconservation.org/what-we-do/tours/edward-steves-homestead-museum

LEAVE YOUR WORRIES BEHIND
AT OUR LADY OF LOURDES GROTTO

San Antonio's Our Lady of Lourdes Grotto is the perfect space to take a deep breath away from life's hustle and bustle. Plus, it's a two-for-one grotto. In addition to the Lourdes grotto, an exact replica of the shrine in France, the Our Lady of Guadalupe Tepeyac de San Antonio place of prayer and devotion is located on top of the Lourdes grotto. Masses at the grotto are Saturdays at 6 p.m.; Sundays at 9 a.m. in English and 11:30 a.m. in Spanish; Mondays through Saturdays at 7 a.m. in English; Mondays through Fridays at noon in Spanish; and a Charismatic Mass at 7 p.m. on Thursdays. The rosary is said at 7:30 p.m. on Mondays and Wednesdays. The Oblate School of Theology's grounds are filled with walking paths, shade trees, outdoor Stations of the Cross, and benches. A large gift shop, filled with reasonably priced books, holy medals, holy cards, and rosaries, is located near the grotto and is open seven days a week from 10 a.m. to 6 p.m.

5712 Blanco Rd., between Oblate and Parade
(210) 342-9864
oblatemissions.org/our-lady-of-lourdes-grotto

VISIT
TEXAS'S ONLY UNESCO WORLD HERITAGE SITE

San Antonio's eighteenth-century Spanish Colonial missions—Concepción, San José, San Juan Capistrano, Espada, and San Antonio de Valero (the Alamo)—are one of only twenty-three USESCO World Heritage Sites in the United States. They share the list with the Grand Canyon, Yellowstone, the Statue of Liberty, and Monticello. In other words, they are a *must-do* thing in San Antonio. Though similar, each mission has its own distinct flavor. Noteworthy items include the rose window and grist mill at San José, the arched doorway and aqueduct at Espada, the cloister at Concepción, the demonstration garden at San Juan, and the shrine and Long Barrack at the Alamo. The National Park Service's visitor center is located at San José, where the film *Gente de Razon* explains life in the 1700s. The Mission Reach, an eight-mile stretch of the River Walk, makes travelling from mission to mission a breeze. You can also hop on board VIA's VIVA #40 Missions route, which runs daily from 8:30 a.m. to 5:30 p.m.

nps.gov/saan/index
thealamo.org

SAUNTER ALONG
SAN PEDRO CREEK CULTURE PARK

San Antonio's 2018 Tricentennial Celebration was not just a giant three-hundredth birthday party. It was also an opportunity for current citizens to leave behind something significant—a legacy—for future generations to enjoy. Thanks to the vision and planning of Bexar County's leaders, the San Pedro Creek Culture Park opened near Columbus Park on the western edge of downtown, transforming an ugly drainage ditch into a restored ecosystem that celebrates San Antonio's vibrant history. Currently, more than 3,900 feet of ADA-accessible walkways allow visitors to stroll past site-specific artwork created by local artists and writers to reveal San Pedro Creek's long history. When all four phases are complete, this linear park will add four miles of walking trails and eleven acres of landscaping to downtown San Antonio.

715 Camaron St.
spccuturepark.com

PAY YOUR RESPECTS
AT SAN FERNANDO CEMETERY

San Fernando Cemetery Number Two covers ninety-two acres of land on San Antonio's West Side. Founded in 1921, the cemetery hosts the remains of Congressman Henry B. González and thousands more of San Antonio's citizens. The cemetery is filled with vintage tombstones that rival the ones in the famous Père Lachaise Cemetery in Paris, where the Doors's Jim Morrison is buried. Strolling through San Fernando and reading the tombstones, the link to our city's history is palpable. At the end of October/beginning of November, the Aztec tradition of the Day of the Dead (El Día de los Muertos), which celebrates the lives of departed loved ones, is alive and well in the Alamo City. At this cemetery and others, you will find family members spiffing up the graves of their friends and relatives.

746 Castroville Rd.
(210) 432-2303
archsa.org/catholic-cemeteries

SAN ANTONIO IS CRAWLING WITH DÍA DE LOS MUERTOS EVENTS FOR YOU TO ENJOY:

- SAY Sí's Muertitos Fest
- The Esperanza Center's Día de los Muertos Celebration
- Market Square's Día de los Muertos Celebration
- La Villita's Día de los Muertos Celebration
- The Guadalupe Cultural Arts Center's Día de los Muertos Celebration

SIT FOR A SPELL
IN SAN FERNANDO CATHEDRAL

Many believe that the Alamo is the heart of San Antonio, but in reality San Fernando Cathedral wears that crown. Built by the Canary Islands settlers in 1738, the first structure was destroyed by fire in 1828. In 1872 its dome fell in, and in 1921 floodwaters reached as high as the Stations of the Cross. Despite all these setbacks, the cathedral, which underwent a major restoration in 2003, remained strong. Jim Bowie was married in San Fernando, and his remains are entombed there along with those of Davy Crockett and William B. Travis. Thanks to the leadership of Phil Hardberger, a former San Antonio mayor, the area in front of San Fernando Cathedral is now a pedestrian-only plaza that leads down to the River Walk. The cathedral and its surrounding area are definitely among my top ten San Antonio must-see destinations. When Pope John Paul II was in San Antonio in the mid-'80s and celebrated Mass at San Fernando, he said that he knew he was in the United States, but he felt that he was in Mexico. He was. The Mexican and Spanish roots of San Antonio are deepest at San Fernando. Don't miss San Antonio I The Saga, a glorious twenty-four-minute, seven-thousand-square-foot multimedia art exhibit of San Antonio's history that is projected onto the cathedral on Tuesdays, Fridays, Saturdays, and Sundays beginning at 9 p.m.

archsa.org/parishes/san-fernando-cathedral

EXPERIENCE THE PASO DE LA MUERTE
(DEATH PASS) AT THE CHARREADA

The San Antonio Asociacion de Charros (horsemen) has been on the banks of the San Antonio River near Mission San Jose since 1947. The association's goal is to pass along a love for the charrería, the grandfather of rodeo. Both male and female teams compete in charreadas, which take place April through November on Sunday afternoons. Admission is $10 for adults and $5 for children. Food and drink are available for purchase in the arena. During the three-hour rodeo, you will experience the "Marcha Zacatecas," where the teams and the queen are presented to the audience and judges; the "Cala," showing the agility of the horses; the charreada, or bull and bronc riding as well as team roping; and finally the "Paso de la Muerte" (death pass), in which the charro rides his horse bareback and attempts to jump on a wild horse and tame it. Now that's something you don't see every day.

6126 Padre Dr.
sacharros.org

LOOKING FOR LOVE?
APPEAL TO ST. ANTHONY DE PADUA

San Antonio is named for St. Anthony of Padua. For those in the know, St. Anthony is the go-to guy for finding lost or stolen items. What you may not know is that St. Anthony is also the go-to guy for finding your true love. In Guatemala, singles flock to area churches on St. Anthony's Feast Day, June 13, to ask him for help finding their better half. It just so happens that I was in Antigua, Guatemala, on St. Anthony's Feast Day back in 1992. The woman I was boarding with sent me to the church across the street to have a chat with St. Anthony and place thirteen coins in his offering box. Is it a coincidence that my boyfriend showed up two weeks later with an engagement ring that sparkled with thirteen diamonds? I don't think so. Residents of and visitors to San Antonio can connect with St. Anthony right here in the Alamo City. St. Anthony de Padua Catholic Church was founded to serve the workers and neighbors of Cementville, the area surrounding the Alamo Cement Company's quarry, home of the current Alamo Quarry Market. Inside the church, which also holds a special devotion to Our Lady of Guadalupe, you'll find a relic of St. Anthony encased in a marble stand. Look below the St. Anthony statue to the left of the altar. The prayer chapel out front is the original 1927 church. Outdoor Stations of the Cross beckon visitors.

102 Lorenz Rd., stanthonydepadua.org

CONNECT WITH NATURE
AT THE SAN ANTONIO
BOTANICAL GARDEN

The San Antonio Botanical Garden is a must-see for both visitors and natives. Even those with the blackest of thumbs will come away hopeful. The thirty-eight-acre spread will give you a taste of Japan, deserts, South Texas, the East Texas Piney Woods, and the Texas Hill Country without having to spend money on gas to get there. A new Family Adventure Garden provides fifteen distinct spaces for unstructured play and exploration. The garden's Bird Watch pavilion, given by Bill, Bob, and Elizabeth Lende in honor of John C. and Sidney Helen Holmgreen, provides a quiet space to observe our feathered friends. Maybe it's because I grew up in Southeast Texas, but the East Texas Piney Woods area is my favorite spot in the garden. (The Japanese Garden runs a close second.) If you have only a limited amount of time to explore, be sure this soothing, pine-scented area is on your agenda. Sit for a spell on the porch of the East Texas Cabin and gaze at the sunning turtles, lounging on logs in the tranquil pond. The garden is open seven days per week and may be reached by VIA's #11B (culture) bus route.

555 Funston Place
(210) 536-1400
sabot.org

EXPERIENCE
THE MAJESTIC PEACEFULNESS OF THE BASILICA OF THE LITTLE FLOWER

San Antonio's Basilica of the National Shrine of the Little Flower is one of only eighty basilicas in the United States. The church was built during the Great Depression and named for Saint Thérèse of Lisieux, and you can't miss its bright yellow spires from Interstate 10 when leaving or entering downtown. Located on the corner of Culebra at Zarzamora, the Roman Catholic church rises majestically above the West Side of San Antonio. Inside, visitors will feel a sense of awe and wonder. St. Thérèse believed that we should do everything in life out of our love for God and our neighbors without expecting any reward or recognition in return. "Miss no single opportunity of making some small sacrifice, here by a smiling look, there by a kindly word; always doing the smallest right and doing it all for love," she said. Daily Masses at the Basilica are at noon and 5:30 p.m. Masses on Saturday are at 8 a.m. and 5:30 p.m. (Vigil). Sunday Masses are at 7:30 a.m., 9 a.m. (Spanish), 11 a.m., 1 p.m., and 6:30 p.m. (Spanish).

1715 N. Zarzamora
(210) 735-9126
littleflowerbasilica.org

MEET THE LIONS AND TIGERS AND BEARS
AT THE SAN ANTONIO ZOO

One of my fondest memories of the San Antonio Zoo is a sleepless night spent camping out with a kinkajou, a nocturnal Brazilian rainforest mammal, and my daughter's Girl Scout troop. I've always thought the San Antonio Zoo is one of the Alamo City's best destinations. The Africa Live! area is a fabulous way to "visit" the African continent to learn about its majestic animals and conservation issues. Other highlights of the fifty-six-acre park include Butterflies! Caterpillar Flight School, Gibbon Forest, Kronkosky's Tiny Tot Nature Spot, TOADally!, Lory Landing, Amazonia, the Hixon Bird House, the Friedrich Aquarium, and the Zootennial Carousel. Seven days a week, you can watch the zookeepers feed condors, elephants, and hippos. In the summer—and truthfully pretty much all year long—I recommend that you get to the zoo early. The animals are friskier in the mornings when it's cooler, and you can enjoy watching them eat their breakfasts. It will take you more than one day to see all nine thousand of the zoo's amphibians, birds, reptiles, and mammals, so grab a map and wear comfortable walking shoes.

3903 N. St. Mary's St.
sazoo.org

STEP INTO HISTORY
AT THREE DOWNTOWN SITES

This is cheating, perhaps, but I'm giving you these sites as a three-for-one item because they are a stone's throw from one another and can be visited in one fell swoop. The zero mile marker for the Old Spanish Trail sits on City Hall's square. This movement was organized in the 1920s to promote a paved highway across the southern portion of the United States. It's now known as Interstate 10. The other zero mile markers are in San Diego, California, and St. Augustine, Florida. Famed short story writer O. Henry—William Sydney Porter—lived in a tiny house on the corner of Dolorosa at Laredo in 1885, when he was twenty-three years old. Two of his stories, "A Fog in Santone" and "The Higher Abdication," are set in the Alamo City. The Casa Navarro State Historic Site was the adobe and limestone home of José Antonio Navarro, a signer of the Declaration of Independence for Texas. Visitors will learn about the life and times of this Tejano patriot.

oldspanishtrailcentennial.com
ohenryhouse.org
visitcasanavarro.com

LEARN
ABOUT COWBOYS, TEXAS WILDLIFE, PREHISTORIC PEOPLE, AND DINOSAURS

A visit to the Witte Museum is a journey through Texas over millions of years. While there, you will marvel at dinosaur skeletons, witness how people lived thousands of years ago, and explore wildlife from the vast regions of Texas in the recently transformed Susan Naylor Center. You will learn about the history and people of the region in the Robert J. and Helen C. Kleberg South Texas Heritage Center. At the H-E-B Body Adventure, you will discover the importance of health IQ, empowerment, and wellness. Treasures of the Witte's collection, including paintings by Julian Onderdonk, Porfirio Salinas, José Arpa, Mary Bonner, and William Aiken Walker, are on display in the B. Naylor Morton Research and Collections Center. Don't miss a Gallery Theater play in the Will Smith Amphitheater or a walk around the six major gardens and riverside landscapes on the beautiful campus. The Witte Museum is where nature, science, and culture meet! Put this Smithsonian-affiliated museum on your must-do list.

3801 Broadway
(210) 357-1900
wittemuseum.org

MARDI GRAS?
SCHMARDI GRAS! ¡VIVA FIESTA!

Fiesta San Antonio is a seventeen-day citywide party every April that offers something for everyone: parades, royalty, performing arts, commemorative medals, arts and crafts, colorful cascarones (confetti eggs), cooking competitions, raspas, and more. Launched in 1891 to pay tribute to the heroes of the Alamo and the Battle of San Jacinto, Fiesta now includes more than one hundred nonprofit organizations coordinating many unique events. More than 75,000 volunteers pitch in to make Fiesta happen. The flagship Battle of Flowers Parade is second in size only to the Tournament of Roses Parade. The Fiesta Flambeau Parade is the nation's largest illuminated night parade, and the Texas Cavaliers River Parade is unlike any other. Floats float. Night in Old San Antonio, Cornyation, the Oyster Bake, the King William Fair, and ninety-six other events make Fiesta something you must experience for yourself. You'll be back for this annual extravaganza! Out-of-towners reserve hotel rooms along the parade routes a year in advance.

facebook.com/fiestasa
fiesta-sa.org

FIND YOUR MUSE
AT SOUTHWEST SCHOOL OF ART

The Southwest School of Art's brochure describes the campus as an urban oasis, but I don't think that quite captures the spirit of the place. After all, SSA is housed in what was once a cloistered convent built in 1851. All the prayers of the Ursuline nuns seeped into the pores of the place, giving it a spiritual air. Pick up a self-guided tour brochure at the center to make sure you hit all of SSA's high points, including the Zilker Courtyard that features the Ruth Johnson Memorial Fountain; the chapel, with its gorgeous stained-glass windows and stunning needlepoint tapestry designed by local artist Zelime Matthews; the convent garden with a grotto dedicated to Our Lady of Lourdes; and the River Garden and its wedding-worthy gazebo. SSA boasts four contemporary art galleries that are free and open to the public. All are open from 9 a.m. to 5 p.m., Mondays through Saturdays, and 11 a.m. to 4 p.m. on Sundays.

300 Augusta
(210) 200-8200
swschool.org

JUMP ON BOARD
VIA'S VIVA BUSES

For the frugal travelers among you, here's a deal that you won't want to miss! For $2.75, you can purchase an all-day VIA bus pass that'll chauffeur you from one San Antonio hot spot to another. VIVA missions (#40) travels from the Alamo to Mission Concepción, Mission San José, Mission San Juan, and Mission Espada, the UNESCO World Heritage sites. VIVA culture (#11A and #11B) voyages from Southtown to the McNay Art Museum, connecting you to parks, theaters, museums, art galleries, and the zoo. VIVA centro (#301) covers the city center from VIA's Centro Plaza to Sunset Station. Highlights include the Tobin Center for the Performing Arts, the Alamo, St. Paul Square, the Henry B. Gonzalez Convention Center, the Briscoe Western Art Museum, and UTSA's downtown campus. You'll be hard pressed to visit all the hot spots in one day, but why not give it a try? If you're in San Antonio without a car, VIA's VIVA routes are the way to go. The one-day pass is also good for unlimited rides on all regular buses, express buses, and streetcars. You can purchase your one-day pass from VIA's online store or through its trip-planning and mobile-ticketing app, VIA goMobile.

viaonlinestore.net

EXPLORE
SAN ANTONIO'S IVORY TOWERS

San Antonio is the seventh largest city in America, and it has more than a dozen institutions of higher learning that befit its size: the Alamo Colleges (Northeast Lakeview College, Northwest Vista College, Palo Alto College, San Antonio College, and St. Philip's College), Our Lady of the Lake University, Trinity University, St. Mary's University, Texas A&M University–San Antonio, University of the Incarnate Word, University of Texas at San Antonio, UT Health San Antonio, and more. Each campus has its own personality, so spend time walking around. Check out the website of each to learn about special happenings and lectures that are open to the public.

Alamo Colleges: alamo.edu

Incarnate Word: uiw.edu

Our Lady of the Lake: ollusa.edu

St. Mary's: stmarytx.edu

Texas A&M–San Antonio: tamusa.edu

Trinity: trinity.edu

University of Texas at San Antonio: utsa.edu

UT Health San Antonio: uthscsa.edu

HONOR
MLK'S LEGACY

Dr. Martin Luther King Jr. surely smiles down from heaven every time he sees the crowd gathered at San Antonio's annual march in his honor. It's one of the largest in the country. Each year on his national holiday, more than 150,000 people gather to stroll a 2.75-mile route along the East Side of San Antonio. What?! Choosing to march rather than sleep in on a holiday? Yes. San Antonio celebrates its diversity. Ivy Taylor, a former mayor who was the first African-American female mayor of a major US city, said: "Dr. King inspired Americans of all colors and creeds to feel that we were part of something bigger, part of an experiment in democracy and freedom that had yet to be fully realized," she said. "He challenged each of us to play a role in fulfilling the promises made by the founding fathers at the creation of the United States of America: 'We hold these truths to be self-evident, that all men are created equal.'" The march reminds each of us to support Dr. King's dream.

sanantonio.gov/mlk

RELEASE YOUR INNER TECHIE
AT GEEKDOM

Geekdom's mission is to "provide an environment where we empower and inspire innovators in order to transform our world for the better." The collaborative coworking space for entrepreneurs, developers, makers, and creatives was founded by Graham Weston of Rackspace and Nick Longo of CoffeeCup Software. It provides geeks and wannabes a chance to mingle and learn from one another and perhaps launch the next big tech innovation. My San Antonio Bloggers group has met at Geekdom a couple of times for all-day workshops, and it's a chill space located in the historic Rand Building downtown. Luddites need not worry. Every member of Geekdom must give one hour a week back to another member or do a workshop once a month on their expertise. In other words, it's their mission to make you more tech savvy. Tours are hosted at noon and 4 p.m., Monday through Friday. Schedule yours today!

110 E. Houston St.
(210) 373-6730
geekdom.com

IMMERSE YOURSELF
IN MILITARY HISTORY AT FORT SAM HOUSTON

My maternal grandfather, a physician, served at Fort Sam Houston during World War II. Years later, my daughter, his great-granddaughter, played her only year of soccer on the fields at Fort Sam. Talk to ten people, and at least one is bound to have a Fort Sam connection. In operation since 1879, Fort Sam is a National Historic Landmark, and it is one of the Army's oldest installations, with more than nine hundred buildings. Geronimo, Teddy Roosevelt, Gen. John J. "Black Jack" Pershing, and President Dwight D. Eisenhower are all part of its history. The Quadrangle, a visitor favorite, is full of deer, peacocks, ducks, and geese that roam beneath an 1876 clock tower. The Quadrangle is open from 9 a.m. to 5 p.m. on weekdays and from noon to 8 p.m. on weekends. Fort Sam's Museum at 2310 Stanley Road is open from 10 a.m. to 4 p.m., Monday through Friday, and from noon to 4 p.m. on Saturday. Bring a photo ID for entrance into Fort Sam, and bring quarters to buy pellets to feed the birds and deer. Admission is free. Enter through the Walters Street visitor gate west of Interstate 35.

Ft. Sam Houston Visitor Center, Building 4179
(210) 221-9205
facebook.com/FSHMuseum

TAKE A SPIN
IN A HORSE-DRAWN CARRIAGE

San Antonio is one of the most romantic cities on the planet. Aside from the San Antonio River Walk, which is perfect for strolling hand-in-hand with your *amor*, the Alamo City also offers horse-drawn carriage rides to take you and your sweetie for *una vuelta* around downtown. The Yellow Rose Carriage Company has been in business since 1982, and it's no coincidence that Valentine was the name of the company's first horse. Lone Star Carriage Company has been in business since 1981, and its slogan is "Let's horse around in San Antonio!" Bluebonnet Carriage Company was founded in 2005, and its mission is to make the ordinary truly extraordinary. According to its website, the "romance" package includes a twenty-minute tour of downtown, a cozy blanket for snuggling, a bouquet of roses, and a box of chocolates. Sign me up! Dark chocolates, please. I'll bring the champagne. You can find the horse-drawn carriages across from the Menger Hotel, adjacent to the Alamo.

yellowrosecarriage.com
lonestarcarriage.com
bluebonnetcarriage.com

CATCH THE STARS
AT THE SCOBEE EDUCATION CENTER
AT SAN ANTONIO COLLEGE

Named for Francis Richard "Dick" Scobee, a former student of SAC who became a US astronaut, the 22,000-square-foot Scobee Education Center gives visitors a hands-on opportunity to experience space. The $12-million center includes the Scobee Planetarium and the Challenger Learning Center. The planetarium is open to the public most Friday evenings, with reasonably priced, age-specific programs for children ages four and above. The Challenger Learning Center offers simulated missions to the International Space Station for middle school-aged students on science- and math-related field trips. The Scobee Education Center also offers free star-gazing parties throughout the year. Its $25,000 telescope in the Charles E. Cheever Jr. Star Tower will bring the stars within your reach.

1819 N. Main Ave.
(210) 486-0100
facebook.com/scobeeplanetarium

GET YOUR GREEN ON
AT ECO CENTRO

Now every day is Earth Day in the Alamo City, thanks to the William R. Sinkin Eco Centro, a sustainability outreach center. Named for a San Antonio College alumnus and clean energy champion, the center's goal is to equip the citizens of this region with information on how to achieve a more sustainable lifestyle. Eco Centro, a 3,100-square-foot LEED-certified building, gives San Antonio residents and visitors a place to gather and learn how to protect and heal our planet. Hands-on classes include water catchment, organic gardening, composting, tree care, green building, vermiculture, and xeriscaping. When you're at Eco Centro, be sure to soak in the sixty-three-foot-long outdoor mural created by Tobin Hill resident Luis Lopez. The artist paid homage to the Native Americans who lived in the area surrounding nearby San Pedro Springs more than twelve thousand years ago.

1802 N. Main Ave.
(210) 486-0417
facebook.com/ecocentro1

AMBLE AROUND
EL MERCADO

El Mercado (Market Square), a downtown landmark within walking distance of the River Walk, is filled with shops, restaurants, and art galleries. Situated across from Milam Park and the Children's Hospital of San Antonio, this outdoor plaza, coined "The Heartbeat of Mexico," hosts a variety of festivals, such as Cinco de Mayo, El Día de Los Muertos, and Fiesta del Mercado, throughout the year. El Mercado boasts of being the largest Mexican market in the United States. Mi Tierra, a Mexican restaurant with a full bar and bakery, has been in business since 1941, and it is open twenty-four hours a day. Don't miss the Mexican fudge. Christmas lights make every day a holiday at Mi Ti's. Add in roaming mariachis and you've got yourself a party. La Margarita Restaurant and Oyster Bar and Viva Villa Taquería are additional El Mercado options for the hungry and thirsty.

marketsquaresa.com

EXPERIENCE SPANISH COLONIAL LIFE
AT THE GOVERNOR'S PALACE

When a friend from Spain visited San Antonio, I made it a point to tour the Spanish Governor's Palace, a National Historic Landmark located across the street from City Hall, with him. Spain's roots in San Antonio are deep. The palace served as the headquarters of the Presidio San Antonio de Bexar's captain and then the home of the Spanish governors. Completed in 1749, it is one of the oldest residences in Texas. Don't think Versailles, though. It's very small by today's mega-mansion standards. Guests can tour the captain's office and home, a living area, a children's bedroom, a dining room, a kitchen, and a loft. My favorite area, however, is the back patio and courtyard. The stone walls, arched patio, and lovely fountain provide a peaceful respite from downtown's hustle and bustle, but the space probably wasn't so peaceful for the criminals who were hanged from the oak trees. In a country that's so new in the grand scheme of things, it's nice to have a piece of history in San Antonio that pre-dates the Declaration of Independence.

105 Plaza de Armas
(210) 224-0601
spanishgovernorspalace.org

MARVEL
IN THE ARCHITECTURE OF THE TOWER LIFE BUILDING

When I moved to San Antonio in 1979, the building that made me feel like I was no longer in a small town but in a big city was the Tower Life Building, which opened in 1929. Designed by famed San Antonio architects Ayres & Ayres, the eight-sided, thirty-story downtown building gave me a New York City vibe. It still does. The building is positioned along the San Antonio River, and I'd often admired its gargoyles while walking along the River Walk, but I'd never been inside the building until I took a downtown walking tour over the holidays. The lobby sported a beautiful, tall Christmas tree, but most noteworthy was its snowflake ceiling. The Tower Life's copper roof, green with patina, gives the building its character, as does its one-hundred-foot flagpole that displays the American flag. When the tower is lit up at night, it demands that you take a look. Go ahead. Look.

310 S. St. Mary's St.
(210) 554-4444
towerlife.com

TOUR PUBLIC ART
ON THE WEST SIDE

Since 1994, San Anto Cultural Arts has identified, trained, and mobilized local artists, both young and old, to create large-scale murals that enliven and help educate the city's urban core. Docent-led or self-guided tours bring the stories, hopes, and dreams of the area's residents to life. The importance of education, *familia*, and Chicano/Chicana culture is on vivid display.

If you don't have time to tour all fifty murals, here are five you should definitely check out:

- *Educación* (1994), 2121 Guadalupe St.
- *Eight Stages of the Life of a Chicana* (1995), 1303 Tampico St.
- *Mano a Mano* (1999), 1927 W. Commerce
- *Piedad* (2003), 1204 Buena Vista
- *Líderes de la Comunidad* (2006), 1204 Buena Vista

2120 El Paso St.
(210) 226-7466
sananto.org/community-mural-program.html

LA GLORIA
Bldg N°3
Matilde Elizondo
Prop
Apr 4 1928

EMBRACE DIVERSITY
AT AN EAST SIDE JEWEL

San Antonio has more than its fair share of performing arts spaces: the Majestic, the Empire, the Tobin Center for the Performing Arts, the Alamodome, the AT&T Center, Trinity University's Laurie Auditorium, the Lila Cockrell Theatre, and more. The Carver Community Cultural Center on San Antonio's East Side, however, may give you the biggest bang for your performing arts buck. Why? The Carver, which emphasizes African and African-American culture, seats six hundred. In a place this size, you are able to see the performers, the costumes, and the sets without binoculars. Check out its annual season lineup. A five-minute cab ride from downtown hotels, the Carver is known for bringing both national and international performers in to celebrate the diverse cultures of our world. For those who are driving themselves, parking is free!

226 N. Hackberry
(210) 207-7211
thecarver.org

LEARN
ABOUT THE CONSEQUENCES OF DISCRIMINATION AND APATHY

Since 1975, the Jewish Federation's Community Relations Council has offered Holocaust education to students of this region. Its mission is to educate the community about the dangers of hatred, prejudice, and apathy. In 2000, the Holocaust Memorial Museum opened its doors to the general public for self-guided tours. School groups and scheduled groups of fifteen or more are given a docent-led tour and the opportunity to speak with a local Holocaust survivor. Admission is free, but donations are encouraged. Learn about the Nazi rise to power, the concentration camps, and American soldiers who liberated the survivors. An outdoor contemplation area memorializes the six million who died.

12500 NW Military Hwy.
(210) 302-6807
hmmsa.org

GET IN TOUCH
WITH YOUR SPIRITUAL SIDE

Although San Antonio's population is one-third Roman Catholic, the religion of the Spaniards who settled here in the early 1700s, Protestant, Jewish, Sikh, Baha'i, Buddhist, Eastern Catholic, Greek Orthodox, Hindu, Muslim, Quaker, and Unitarian congregations abound to help you develop your personal value system and explore the meaning of life.

Baha'i: sanantoniobahai.org

Buddhist: sanantonio.shambhala.org, sanantoniozen.org, tbcwp.org, facebook.com/sabuddhisttemple

Eastern Catholic: stgeorgesa.org

Jewish: jfsatx.org/community-directory

Greek Orthodox: stsophiagoc.org

Hindu: hindutemplesatx.org

Muslim: icsaonline.org

Nondenominational: celebrationcircle.org

Protestant: churches-in.com/texas/San+Antonio

Quaker: sanantonioquakers.org

Roman Catholic: archsa.org/parishes

Sikh: sikhcentersa.org

Unitarian: uusat.org

● ●

TAKE IN A PERFORMANCE
OR TAKE A CLASS AT THE GUADALUPE

Founded in 1980 in the historic 1940 Teatro Guadalupe that sits deep in the heart of San Antonio's West Side, the Guadalupe Cultural Arts Center hosts a treasure trove of Chicano/Chicana arts programming and classes in six major areas: visual arts, music, literature, film, theater, and dance. I took a writing class at the Guadalupe from the then-unknown Sandra Cisneros not long after her book *The House on Mango Street* was published. Great teacher. Great class. The San Antonio CineFestival, the Tejano Conjunto Festival, the Guadalupe Dance Company, Hecho a Mano Outdoor Market, and more bring Hispanic heritage and culture to life throughout the year. While you're there, don't miss *La Veladora of Our Lady of Guadalupe*, a forty-foot outdoor mosaic sculpture by local artist Jesse Treviño, who also designed the mosaic mural on the Children's Hospital of San Antonio across from El Mercado and the painted mural in San Antonio's Central Library.

723 S. Brazos St.
(210) 271-3151
guadalupeculturalarts.org

CRUISE ALONG THE SAN ANTONIO RIVER
TO SOAK UP THE CITY'S HISTORY

Venice, Italy, isn't the only city you can traverse by boat. San Antonio has its own shuttle service and tours to spirit you away. Knowledgeable drivers will give you the 411 on local points of interest. Open from 9 a.m. to 10 p.m. daily, GO RIO's narrated, thirty-five-minute cruises cost $12 per person and travel along the horseshoe bend of the river. Its shuttle service offers a twenty-four-hour pass for $16 at thirteen stops downtown and along the Museum Reach. All of the river barges are ADA accessible. Charters are available for groups, corporate outings, and dinners. Close to fifty restaurants provide dinner cruises that can be reserved by the seat. My absolute favorite time of year to jump on a cruise is during the holidays from the day after Thanksgiving through the first part of January. Twinkling colored lights in trees along the river create a magical fairyland that will transport you into another dimension.

(210) 227-4746
goriocruises.com

RAMBLE THROUGH
EAST SIDE CEMETERIES

In 1853, the City of San Antonio purchased twenty acres east of downtown to house the final remains of San Antonio's citizens. By 1904, thirty-one public, private, religious, fraternal, and military cemeteries covered more than 103 acres. Many of San Antonio's "Who's Who" are buried in these cemeteries: Clara Driscoll and Adina De Zavala, saviors of the Alamo; John Lang Sinclair, songwriter of "The Eyes of Texas"; Julian Onderdonk, Texas landscape artist; Samuel Augustus Maverick, a lawyer, politician, and signer of the Texas Declaration of Independence; Alfred Giles, architect; Thomas Claiborne Frost, founder of Frost Bank; Harry M. Wurzbach, congressman; and Robert H. H. Hugman, concept architect of the San Antonio River Walk, to name a few. The National Cemetery contains the remains of more than three hundred Buffalo Soldiers, African Americans who served during the Indian Wars. One of the more colorful residents of the East Side cemeteries is Sandra West, the widow of oilman Ike West Jr. Sandra asked to be buried dressed in a lace nightgown inside her cherished 1964 baby blue Ferrari "with the seat slanted comfortably," and she was.

517 Paso Hondo St.
cem.va.gov/cems/nchp/sanantonio.asp

PAY A VISIT
TO THE PAINTED CHURCHES

While working on the second edition of this book, I asked the members of the Professional Tour Guide Association of San Antonio for their input. One of its members asked if I knew about the three painted churches downtown. I guessed St. Joseph, St. Mary, and San Fernando. She said that the first two were correct, but San Fernando didn't fit the profile. German and Czech immigrants who arrived in Texas in the mid-1800s built the painted churches. Immaculate Heart of Mary, located south of Market Square, is number three. Built by the Claretian Missionaries in 1912, the Byzantine- and Romanesque-style church is filled with lofty arches set atop sturdy pillars. The real showstopper, however, is the church's interior paint. The shade of blue on the Immaculate Heart of Mary's walls and ceiling is one of the prettiest I've ever seen. It's the same green-blue that graces Our Lady of Guadalupe's mantle (*tilma*). Besides its striking interior, the church houses the original bell that broadcast the fall of the Alamo on March 6, 1836, from San Fernando Cathedral. IHM inherited the bell after San Fernando purchased four new bells for its towers in 1904.

DON'T MISS THESE THREE BEAUTIES!

Immaculate Heart of Mary
617 S. Santa Rosa Ave.
ihmsatx.org

St. Joseph Catholic Church
623 E. Commerce St.
stjsa.org

St. Mary
202 N. St. Mary's St.
archsa.org/parishes/st.-mary

FOSTER A LIFETIME LOVE OF LEARNING
AT THE DOSEUM

The last time I had visited "San Antonio's museum for kids" was in 2002, when it was located on Houston Street and my daughter was in preschool. So I was intrigued by all the buzz in my bloggers group from moms with children in the zero-to-ten age range. "It's our new favorite place," said one. "We *love* it!" said another. So I had to go see it for myself, and I now understand all the accolades. It's awesome, and it's *huge* (65,000 square feet of indoor space and 39,000 square feet of outdoor space). Even though I am not a child, I had fun skipping up the piano-key stairs, pretending that I was a member of the stranded Robinson family in the whimsical outdoor tree house, and learning about how different lights change the colors that we see. I also enjoyed chatting with a young girl who was happily engaged in creating a spy kitty mask in the DoSeum's art studio. The arts, science, technology, engineering, math, and literacy are all featured in this $47-million hands-on museum.

2800 Broadway
(210) 212-4453
thedoseum.org

VISIT THE COUNTY SEAT
OF SAN ANTONIO DE BÉXAR

The 1896 Romanesque Revival-style Bexar (pronounced "bear") County Courthouse sits on the edge of Main Plaza, its Texas granite and red sandstone exterior an eye-catching contrast to the limestone of nearby San Fernando Cathedral. A seven-story cupula shaped like a beehive beckons visitors to this Texas Historic Landmark that's also listed on the National Register of Historic Places. A $23-million multi-year renovation completed in 2015 has the seat of county government restored to architect James Riely Gordon's original vision, including a two-story district courtroom with coffered ceilings, gilded plaster moldings and capitals, longleaf pine floors, and fifteen decorative windows. Don't forget to look down, though, when you're in the courthouse. The Mission tile floors are a thing of beauty.

100 Dolorosa
(210) 335-2011
bexar.org

RECHARGE YOUR *QI* (LIFE FORCE)
ON THE SPIRIT REACH OF THE SAN ANTONIO RIVER

The headwaters of the San Antonio River are located in a protected fifty-three-acre sanctuary established by the Sisters of Charity of the Incarnate Word, who came to San Antonio in 1869 to care for victims of a massive cholera epidemic. The native people called the springs Yanaguana, a Coahuiltecan word that means Spirit Waters, and they once gushed twenty feet into the air. Located near the center of San Antonio, this sanctuary provides city-weary visitors a chance to meander along trails and connect with mighty oak trees, native plants, and wildlife that includes more than one hundred species of birds. The sanctuary also provides volunteers an opportunity to restore the ecosystem health of this sacred space. Parking is ticket-free on Fridays, Saturdays, and Sundays near the University of the Incarnate Word's baseball fields. Look for the sanctuary entrance near the headwaters's toolshed.

4503 Broadway (GPS: 29.4698, –98.4708)
(210) 828-2224, ext. 280
headwaters-iw.org

• •

TAKE IN SAN ANTONIO'S
TRICENTENNIAL PUBLIC ART

To celebrate its founding by Spanish missionaries in 1718, San Antonio threw itself party after party throughout 2018. Fortunately, not all the celebrations were ephemeral. Public art dedicated during the Tricentennial now permanently graces our fair city. Here are five of my favorites:

- *¡Adelante San Antonio!*, a three-part mural at the San Antonio International Airport created by local artists Suzy González and Michael Menchaca, chronicles San Antonio's three-hundred-year history and culture.

- *Alas de México* (*Wings of Mexico*) by Mexican artist Jorge Marín is a gift from the citizens of Mexico City to the citizens of San Antonio. Located near the base of Hemisfair Tower, it has quickly become one of the most Instagrammed spots in San Antonio.

- *San Antonio Street Art Initiative*, located under Interstate 35 at Quincy/St. Mary's, features colorful images by sixteen local artists on twenty-foot-tall concrete freeway columns. Perfect for photographs.

- *Tribute to Freedom* by local artist George Schroeder is the tallest metal sculpture in Texas. Located outside Joint Base San Antonio–Lackland, the artwork pays tribute to all five branches of the US Armed Forces, fitting for "Military City USA," a registered trademark of the City of San Antonio.

- *Tricentennial Clock*, a kinetic sculpture by Ansen Seale, is in the 1883 Roatzch-Griesenbeck-Arciniega House in the shadow of the Alamodome. The work highlights the passage of time into the future while honoring the past.

● ●

FOOD AND DRINK

ENJOY A BIRD'S-EYE HAPPY HOUR
FROM THE TOWER OF THE AMERICAS

My love affair with San Antonio began in 1968 when my parents took one of my brothers and me to the World's Fair, Hemisfair, to soak up the region's confluence of civilizations and celebrate San Antonio's 250th birthday. All these years later, there's even more reason to love San Antonio. Name another place where you can enjoy a $6 glass of wine or $5 beer at the top of the city's tallest building, with a breathtaking 360-degree view. I thought so. Happy Hour at the Tower of the Americas is Monday through Friday from 4:30 p.m. to 7 p.m. Make sure you get in the elevator line for the Chart House Restaurant, which also happens to be a romantic dinner destination. Another queue is for the observation deck. O'Neil Ford, famed local architect, designed the 622-foot tower, the tallest building in San Antonio. Ford also designed Trinity University's tower and campus. Be sure to snap a picture of yourself at *Alas de México* (*Wings of Mexico*), a Tricentennial public art piece, near the base of the tower.

739 E. César E. Chávez Blvd.
(210) 223-3101
toweroftheamericas.com

QUENCH YOUR THIRST
AT THE LONGEST BAR IN TEXAS

When my husband and I bellied up to the one-hundred-foot wooden bar at The Esquire Tavern, the gentleman standing next to us said that he owns a T-shirt from the establishment's earlier days that reads, "I got frisked at The Esquire." Frisking no longer takes place, but the colorful history of this place makes for interesting conversation. Founded in 1933 on the day that Prohibition was recalled, The Esquire has been a mainstay of downtown San Antonio's thirsty crowd for more than eighty years. The owners claim that it's the oldest bar on the San Antonio River Walk, and who can disprove them? The Esquire bills itself as a gastro pub that serves comfort foods. It is also a big force behind San Antonio's cocktail culture, so figure out ahead of time whether you want your aperitif shaken or stirred.

155 E. Commerce St.
(210) 222-2521
esquiretavern-sa.com

BECOME A BREAKFAST TACO BELIEVER

Whenever I travel outside of San Antonio, I most enjoy returning home to breakfast tacos. Those who live here get it. Those who don't live here don't know what they're missing. San Antonio is not only the capital of Tex-Mex cuisine but also the undisputed capital of breakfast tacos. We have an embarrassment of riches. Corn or flour tortillas? Eggs or not? Potatoes? Bacon, ham, or sausage? With or without cheese? Barbacoa? Guacamole? So many options. Personally, I find a migas taco on a corn tortilla with cheese and the perfect amount of *salsa quemada* to be a life-affirming experience.

A BAKER'S DOZEN OF BREAKFAST TACO PICKS

Blue Moon Café
facebook.com/Blue-Moon-Cafe-117889961570317

Maria's Café
facebook.com/mariascafe.ann

Mendez Café
facebook.com/pages/Mendez-Cafe/1401964606743670

El Milagrito Café
elmilagritocafe.com

Panchito's Mexican Restaurant
panchitos.net

Paulina's Mexican Restaurant
facebook.com/Paulinas-Mexican-Restaurant-177177872329268

Pete's Tako House
petestakohouse.com

Sabor de Mexico
facebook.com/pages/Sabor-De-Mexico/114055505293224

Taco Cabana
tacocabana.com

Taco Garage
tacogarage.com

Taco House
facebook.com/Taco-House-117574761601921

Taco Taco Café
tacotacosa.com

Teka Molino
tekamolino.com

GET ON BOARD
THE BBQ WAGON

Sliced beef brisket is one place where my family falls off the eat-no-red-meat wagon. When it comes to brisket that's been smoked to perfection and sliced into thin, toothsome strips, our willpower fades away. Sliced beef BBQ must be woven into native Texans' DNA, so we're helpless against its powerful pull. Smoked brisket should be acknowledged for the best smell the Alamo City produces. If only it could be bottled and sold! You could do a two-week vacation in San Antonio and not hit all the BBQ joints in town, but you could try!

BBQ RECOMMENDATIONS

2M Smokehouse
2msmokehouse.com

Augie's Barbed Wire
augiesbbq.com

B&B Smokehouse
bbsmokehouse.com

B&D Ice House
banddicehouse.com

Barbecue Station
barbecuestation.com

Big Bib BBQ
thebigbib.com

Bill Miller Bar-B-Q
billmillerbbq.com

Blanco BBQ
blancobbq.com

Bolner's Meat Company
bolnersmeatmarket.com

Ed's Smok-N-Q
facebook.com/pages/Eds-Smok-N-Q/982211258562306

The Granary 'Cue and Brew
thegranarysa.com

Rudy's Country Store and Bar-B-Q
rudysbbq.com

The Smokehouse
thesmokehousebbqsa.com

Smoke Shack
smokeshacksa.com

LEAVE NO PALETA UNTRIED

When the temperature tops one hundred degrees, load the biggest ice chest you own into your car or onto a VIA bus and head on over to El Paraiso Ice Cream for its fruit bars, also known as *paletas*. Founded in 1984, this family-owned business was the first paleta factory in San Antonio, according to Azucena Flores, daughter of Jose and Maria Flores, the owners. Daughters Maggie and Elizabeth and son Jose Jr. also work at the factory and in the shop, along with various uncles and cousins. The Floreses produce more than ten thousand paletas a day. Strawberry is their number-one seller, followed by lemon. Coconut and chocolate are tied for third, and vanilla/raisin comes in fourth. Other flavors include banana, mango, tamarind, pecan, pineapple, piña colada, horchata, cantaloupe, cookies and cream, watermelon, pickles, lucas (sweet and sour), cheesecake, and coffee cappuccino. One paleta will set you back fifty cents. If you buy twenty-six at a time, you'll pay forty-six cents per paleta. You'll have a hard time finding a sweeter deal in all of the Alamo City!

1934 Fredericksburg Rd.
(210) 737-8101
elparaisoicecream.com

HEAD TO HAWX
FOR THE ULTIMATE BURGER AND FRIES

Those who are devout followers of my blog know that I have a particular weakness for French fries. They are my Achilles heel. Hawx Burger Bar *rocks* at French fries. Order the simply salted fries and/or the Asiago truffle fries and die happy. Hawx claims to make the perfect burger, and you really can't argue with the assertion. Order one of the double-ground Angus Chuck beef burgers served on a freshly baked brioche bun piled to your heart's content, and you'll soon endorse the claim. The Blue Moon beer-battered jalapeño roulette—the seeds are left in *one* of the jalapeños—and Buffalo wings are also tasty. My husband gives the fried pickle spears a thumbs-up. Hawx has lunch specials every day from 11 a.m. until 3 p.m. Its all-day happy hour includes $5 cocktails seven days per week. Hawx's covered outdoor patio is inviting, and its large, movie-theater-sized indoor screen is the perfect place to catch a favorite team and sip a handcrafted cocktail or draft beer.

2603 Vance Jackson
700 E. Sonterra Blvd., Ste. 318
hawxburgerbar.com

SAVOR SAN ANTONIO'S COMIDA TÍPICA:
BARBACOA AND BIG RED

Barbacoa, slow-cooked beef cheeks, and Big Red, a sugary-sweet bright red soft drink, is a favorite meal here in San Antonio. Ask any native their go-to weekend meal, and chances are they'll tell you barbacoa and Big Red. There's even an annual Barbacoa and Big Red Festival. These ten establishments cook their barbacoa on site. Some cook it throughout the week. Others cook it only on the weekends. Order all meat or mixed (meat with fat) with a side of tortillas and a Big Red. Give Randy Garibay's song "Barbacoa Blues" a listen while you dig in.

Adelita
adelitatamales.com

Culebra Meat Market
culebrameatmarkets.com

Del Rio
delriotortillas.com

Martinez
facebook.com/Martinez-Barbacoa-Y-Tamales-121608857849855

El Milagrito Café
elmilagritocafe.com

Panchito's
panchitos.net

Rios (seventeen locations)/Treviño's (four locations)

Taqueria Datapoint
facebook.com/pages/category/Mexican-Restaurant/Taqueria-Datapoint-374205566057960

Tellez
facebook.com/Tellez-Tamales-Barbacoa-115721145123658

Tommy's
mytommys.com

TOAST TO YOUR GOOD HEALTH
AT SAN ANTONIO'S BEER GARDENS

You often hear both Spanish and English spoken on the streets of San Antonio. We are proud of our dual-language skills, which go back for generations. If you'd been a resident of the Alamo City in the second half of the nineteenth century, you would also have heard German. From 1847 to 1861, more than seven thousand German immigrants moved to San Antonio, making up one-third of the county's population at the time. The German-English School, now used as an event venue at the Marriott Plaza San Antonio hotel, taught English, German, Spanish, writing, poetry, history, arithmetic, algebra, sewing, and singing to local children from 1858 to 1893, according to the Texas State Historical Association. Beethoven Maennerchor, one of the oldest German singing societies in Texas, was founded in 1867. First Fridays, Gartenfest concerts, Fiesta, Oktoberfest, and all the events that draw crowds to the famous Beethoven Biergarten keep patrons coming back each week. It's the dedicated volunteers and members who incorporate Beethoven into their lives—to work the food line, man the parking lot, prep the food, and pour German beer from their taps—that make Beethoven Halle's Biergarten a place you want to hang out. Beethoven is open Tuesday through Saturday from 4 p.m. until midnight. Other San Antonio beer gardens/ice houses to try include Burleson Yard Beer Garden, The Friendly Spot, Bier Garten, La Tuna, Alamo Beer Hall, M. K. Davis, and VFW Post 76.

Alamo Beer Hall
alamobeer.com

Beethoven Halle Biergarten
beethovenmaennerchor.com/club-room

Bier Garten
biergartenriverwalk.com

Burleson Yard Beer Garden
facebook.com/BurlesonYard

The Friendly Spot
thefriendlyspot.com

La Tuna
latunasa.com

M. K. Davis
mkdavisrestaurant.com

VFW Post 76
vfwpost76ontheriverwalk.org

GRAZE YOUR WAY
ACROSS CENTRAL MARKET

Central Market is the H-E-B grocery store chain's gift to San Antonio's citizens and visitors. Just walking into Central Market makes me happy. Buying a bar of dark chocolate with crystallized ginger makes me even happier. Taking in the abundance of fresh-cut flowers and the stunning variety of fruits and vegetables practically makes me swoon. A wonderful thing about Central Market is that you can snack your way across continents for free. (I'm a Spanish cheese addict, I admit.) Everyone in your party will be sure to find something wonderful to eat and drink. Choosing will be the problem; the selection is tremendous. The store also features chef-prepared dinners for two that are packaged to go for $15 or less. How great is that? While you're in the store, pick up something to bring home that'll remind you of your fabulous trip to San Antonio: a package or two of flour tortillas, Texas BBQ sauce, or pecan-flavored coffee called "Taste of San Antonio," for example.

4821 Broadway
(210) 368-8600
centralmarket.com

DO THE TIME WARP
AT DEWESE'S TIP TOP CAFÉ

My husband and I met a friend who graduated from nearby Thomas Jefferson High School in 1960 for dinner at DeWese's Tip Top Café. When we got to the restaurant, Tony said, "Welcome to the time warp." In all the years he's been eating at the Tip Top, it hasn't changed. Why ruin a good thing? Winnie and Pappy DeWese started the restaurant in 1938, and their granddaughter, Linda DeWese, carried it on for many years until her retirement in 2016. It gives its loyal customers what they crave: tried-and-true comfort food. Tony ordered a chiliburger with cheese and a side of the over-the-top onion rings. My husband ordered the famous chicken-fried steak, and I ordered the grilled tilapia. All the food was tasty, but the onion rings alone are worth the trip. Like Earl Abel's and the Pig Stand, two other San Antonio time warp restaurants, the Tip Top has pies galore to top off your meal. Or, if you just want a little something sweet, pick up an Aunt Aggie De's Praline or two when you're checking out. They've been named the Official Best Gourmet Praline and Pecan Candy in Texas.

2814 Fredericksburg Rd.
(210) 732-0191
facebook.com/tiptopcafesanantonio

TRAVEL VICARIOUSLY
IN SAN ANTONIO, TEXAS

You won't need a passport to enjoy international cuisine in San Antonio, which is fast becoming one of America's leading culinary capitals. Give the food at these international establishments a taste. Bon appétit!

Berbere Ethiopian Cuisine (Ethopia)
berbereethiopian.com

Carmens de la Calle (Spain)
carmensdelacalle.com

Chico's Bakery (Mexico)
facebook.com/Chicos-Bakery-478025115911789

Demo's Greek Food (Greece)
demosgreekfood.com

Frederick's (France)
frederickssa.com

La Frite Belgian Bistro (Belgium)
lafritesa.com

The Frutería (Mexico)
chefjohnnyhernandez.com/restaurants/fruteria-southtown

Golden Wok (China)
goldenwoksa.com

Hot Joy (Asian fusion)
hotjoysa.com

Hung Fong Chinese Restaurant (China)
facebook.com/hungfongsa

India Oven (India)
indiaovensa.com

Jerusalem Grill (Middle East)
jerusalemgrill.net

Moshe's Golden Falafel (Israel)
facebook.com/pages/moshes-golden-falafel/451837781660856

Niki's Tokyo Inn (Japan)
facebook.com/nikis.tokyo.inn

Paesano's (Italy)
paesanos.com

Paloma Blanca (Mexico)
palomablanca.net

Pasha Mediterranean Grill (Mediterranean)
gopasha.com

Schilo's Delicatessen (Germany)
schilos.com

Seoul Asian Market (Korea)
seoulasianmarket.com

Simi's India Cuisine (India)
simisindiacuisine.com

Thai Dee (Thailand)
thaideesa.com

TASTE THE BEST
OF TEX-MEX CUISINE

People who've left San Antonio never fail to lament the lack of excellent Tex-Mex food in their new city. The first thing they do when they get back to San Antonio is visit their favorite restaurants. Enchiladas, carne guisada, chalupas, fajitas, refried beans, rice, nachos, flautas, salsa and chips, tacos al pastor, queso, guacamole . . . you can't go wrong!

EAT YOUR WAY ACROSS SAN ANTONIO

Los Barrios
losbarriosrestaurant.com

Blanco Café
facebook.com/blancocafesa

El Bucanero
el-bucanero.com

Casa Rio
casa-rio.com

Don Pedro
donpedro.net

La Fogata
lafogata.com

La Fonda on Main
lafondaonmain.com

Garcia's Mexican Food
www.facebook.com/garcias-mexican-food-133549451128

Mama Margie's
mamamargies.com

Nicha's Comida Mexicana
nichas.com

Rosario's
rosariossa.com

Teka Molino
tekamolino.com

SIT YOURSELF DOWN
AT A TABLE WITH A VIEW

The restaurants on San Antonio's famed River Walk are plentiful. With help from my fellow San Antonio bloggers, the following list was crafted for your dining pleasure. Romance is optional but encouraged.

Ácenar
acenar.com

Biga on the Banks
biga.com

Boudro's Texas Bistro
boudros.com

Las Canarias
omnihotels.com/hotels/san-antonio-la-mansion-del-rio/dining/
las-canarias

Casa Rio
casa-rio.com

Dorrego's
dorregos.com

Fig Tree Restaurant
dine.figtreerestaurant.com

Little Rhein Steak House
dine.littlerheinsteakhouse.com

Ocho
havanasanantonio.com/restaurant-and-bar/ocho

Ostra
omnihotels.com/hotels/san-antonio-mokara/dining/ostra

Paesano's
paesanosriverwalk.com

Las Ramblas
thehotelcontessa.com/san_antonio_restaurant

Range
rangesa.com

LIVE LA VIDA LOCA(VORE)

The locavore movement—eating food that's grown within a hundred-mile radius of where it is purchased—is a national phenomenon that was dreamed up by three San Francisco-area women in 2005. Being a locavore helps reduce greenhouse gas emissions and supports local farmers. Plus, the food tastes great. It isn't processed, and most is organic. San Antonio chefs have jumped on board the locavore movement. Here are six restaurants that make their Mother (Earth) proud:

5 Points Local
5pointslocal.com

Cured
curedatpearl.com

The Good Kind
eatgoodkind.com

Pharm Table
pharmtable.com

Restaurant Gwendolyn
restaurantgwendolyn.com

Southerleigh
southerleigh.com

FIND FOODIE TREASURES
AT THE PEARL

When the Culinary Institute of America opened up a branch in San Antonio at the former Pearl Brewery, a twenty-two-acre site along the Museum Reach of the San Antonio River, the food scene in San Antonio exploded. The CIA's student-staffed restaurant, Savor, allows guests to build a customized three- or four-course meal. Add Bakery Lorraine, The Bar at Bottling Department, Blue Box Bar, Boiler House, Botika, Bud's Southern Rotisserie, Cured, Fletcher's Hamburgers, La Gloria, The Good Kind, The Granary 'Cue and Brew, Green, High Street Wine Company, Jazz TX, Larder, Lick Honest Ice Creams, Local Coffee, Maybelle's Donuts, Southerleigh, Sternewirth, Supper, and Tenko Ramen to Pearl's growing list of restaurants, bakeries, cafés, and bars, and choosing where to eat becomes a difficult decision. As if that weren't enough, farmers and foodies within a 150-mile radius of the Alamo City set up booths filled with vegetables, fresh eggs, cut flowers, baked goods, herbs, cheeses, bison, coffee, chocolates, lavender, and more every Saturday from 9 a.m. until 1 p.m. and Sunday from 10 a.m. until 2 p.m. Rain or shine.

303 Pearl Pkwy.
(210) 212-7260
atpearl.com/food

GRAB A SLICE
(OR TWO OR THREE) OF PIZZA

San Antonio's Italian heritage is deeper than most realize. The local Christopher Columbus Italian Society was chartered in 1890, and San Francesco di Paola Catholic Church was built in 1927 at 205 Piazza Italia off of downtown's Martin Street. Even if you don't have an ounce of Italian blood in you, we're all Italian when it comes to pizza. Here's an alpha-ordered list of a dozen local establishments that will make your life *molto bene!*

Barbaro
barbarosanantonio.com

Big Lou's Pizza
biglouspizza-satx.com

Braza Brava Pizza Napoletana
facebook.com/brazabrava

Capo's Pizzeria
capospizzasa.com

Deco Pizzeria
decopizza.com

Dough Pizzeria Napoletana
doughpizzeria.com

Florio's New York Style Pizza
facebook.com/Florios-Pizza-120473217964539

Il Forno
ilfornosa.com

Guillermo's
guillermosdowntown.com

Julian's Italian Pizzeria and Kitchen
julianspizzeria.com

Sorrento's Italiano Ristoranti
sorrentopizzeria.com

Stella Public House
stellapublichouse.com

SAVOR THE SKYLINE
AND ENJOY A BIEN FRÍA (COLD ONE)

The Hays Street Bridge, a Texas Historic Civil Engineering Landmark built in 1881, spent the first part of its life spanning the Nueces River west of Uvalde. It was later moved to San Antonio and erected in 1910 to provide a railroad-track-free crossing from the East Side of San Antonio to downtown. The bridge, composed of two wrought iron truss spans, was closed in 1982 for safety reasons. It re-opened to pedestrian and bicycle traffic in 2010, one hundred years after it made its San Antonio debut, thanks to the Herculean efforts of the Hays Street Bridge Restoration Group. Photo opportunities abound at this East Side landmark, so bring a camera. After you're done soaking up the views of downtown San Antonio, treat yourself to a locally brewed Alamo beer just beneath the bridge. Alamo's beer garden and beer hall are open daily to the public and offer live music and food trucks. Give "Beer, Bacon, and Bingo" a try on Thursday nights from 6:30 to 8:30!

803 N. Cherry St.
facebook.com/hays-street-bridge-151580447463

SIP A BREW OR TWO
AT VFW POST 76, THE OLDEST IN TEXAS

Even though the VFW Post 76 is the oldest in Texas and was founded by veterans of the Spanish-American War, it was hidden from sight until the Museum Reach opened in 2009. The post was one of San Antonio's best-kept secrets. Not anymore. Strolling along the River Walk from downtown toward the San Antonio Museum of Art or from the Pearl toward downtown, natives and visitors encounter the majestic 1902 Victorian home nestled along the banks of the San Antonio River. On a Friday or Saturday night, the festive crowd and live music will draw you in. The post's canteen is open daily. You don't have to be a veteran to enter VFW Post 76 or to purchase a brew, but you will have the opportunity to rub elbows with veterans of World War II, Korea, Vietnam, the Persian Gulf, and Afghanistan and thank them for their service.

10 Tenth St.
(210) 223-4581
vfwpost76ontheriverwalk.org

TREAT YOURSELF AND YOUR SWEETIE
TO A ROMANTIC REPAST

San Antonio is the most romantic city in the United States, so it's no surprise that the Alamo City has a surfeit of seductive restaurants to help turn up the heat in both new and established relationships. I asked my fellow San Antonio bloggers for their top romantic restaurants, and we came up with this list of swoon-worthy favorites.

Azúca
azuca.net

Battalion
battalionsa.com

Bella on Houston
bellaonhouston.com

Bliss
foodisbliss.com

Bohanan's
bohanans.com

Cappy's
cappysrestaurant.com

The Grey Moss Inn Restaurant
greymossrestaurantthelotestx.com

Little Italy
littleitalyrestaurantmenu.com

Rebelle
rebellesa.com

Tong's Thai Restaurant
tongsthai.com

Zinc Bistro and Bar
zincwine.com

CRUISE ART GALLERIES, HISTORIC HOMES, AND GREAT EATS IN SOUTHTOWN

Southtown, the neighborhood just south of downtown, came onto my radar when the Blue Star Contemporary Art Museum got its start in a warehouse along the San Antonio River back in 1986. H-E-B relocated its corporate headquarters to the area in 1985, San Angel Folk Art Gallery came along in 1989, and then came the expansion of the King William Fair during Fiesta, revitalization of King William's historic homes, First Friday art walks, the Blue Star Brewing Company, and you get the idea. Southtown was abuzz, and it still is. In addition to having arts destinations and historic homes, this part of town is becoming known as a foodie paradise. People who live in the 'hood recommend the following culinary establishments.

Feast
feastsa.com

The Guenther House
guentherhouse.com

Liberty Bar
liberty-bar.com

Madhatters Tea House & Café
madhatterstea.com

Tito's Mexican Restaurant
titosrestaurant.com

La Tuna Grill and La Tuna Icehouse
latunagrill.com

DON'T BE LIKE PRESIDENT FORD!
REMOVE THE HUSK

Even though I grew up in Southeast Texas where Latino anything was scarce, I was raised by parents who loved traveling to Mexico and loved Mexican food. Because of this childhood experience, I pick up a dozen tamales now and again to bring home to my own family. San Antonio, unlike my birthplace, is covered with tamale vendors. In the more than thirty years I've lived here, I've tried quite a few. My favorite tamales, however, come from Adelita Tamales & Tortilla Factory. Four generations of the Borrego family and their employees have been making tamales, tortillas, chips, buñuelos, and more since 1938. For $8.25, you can get a dozen bean and jalapeño tamales to go. Pork or pork with jalapeño will run you $8.75, and a dozen chicken tamales are $9. Pork tamales are their best sellers. All the ingredients are sourced from Texas. Every three months, thirty thousand pounds of corn from LaCoste is delivered to their silo. Inside the factory, the corn is cooked in lime water before being ground by volcanic stone. Their masa is the real deal, and you can taste the difference in their tamales.

1130 Fresno
(210) 733-5352
adelitatamales.com

STEP BACK IN TIME
AT SAN ANTONIO'S OLDEST BAR

The Menger Bar at the Menger Hotel is the oldest continuously operating saloon in San Antonio, according to a plaque outside its front door, which is a stone's throw from the Alamo. Built in 1887, it was an exact replica of London's House of Lords Pub, and former president Teddy Roosevelt enlisted his Rough Riders here in 1898 for the Spanish-American War. With a maximum occupancy of sixty-five, the bar is extremely intimate. Memorabilia from the First Texas Cavalry on the Border (1916–1917) are on display, along with a giant moose head and drawings of Roosevelt. Ask the bartender for a whiskey, and raise a glass to Roosevelt for prioritizing and expanding America's national park system.

204 Alamo Plaza
(210) 223-4361
mengerhotel.com/restaurants

MUSIC AND ENTERTAINMENT

CATCH A SHOW
AT THE TOBIN CENTER FOR THE PERFORMING ARTS

The Tobin Center is home to three of San Antonio's premier performing arts groups: the San Antonio Symphony, Ballet San Antonio, and Opera San Antonio. With another four resident performing arts organizations in its stable and a super-sized list of outside talent, the Tobin offers something for everyone. Located in downtown San Antonio along the Museum Reach of the River Walk, the Tobin Center was transformed from the Municipal Auditorium into its current $203-million incarnation with three separate venues: the H-E-B Performance Hall, with seats for 1,746; the Carlos Alvarez Studio Theater, a smaller space with up to three hundred seats; and the River Walk Plaza, an outdoor amphitheater that has space for twelve hundred standing or six hundred seated along with a thirty-two-foot video wall that allows events inside to be simulcast outside. At night, the Tobin's Gehry-like metal skin, the AT&T Sky Wall, lights up the center's silhouette, giving those of us who are crazy for San Antonio's annual Christmas lights on the River Walk a year-round fix.

100 Auditorium Circle
(210) 223-8624
tobincenter.org

TRANSPORT YOURSELF
INTO ANOTHER WORLD AT THE MAJESTIC THEATRE

Some of the best concerts I've ever attended were in the Majestic Theatre: Stevie Ray Vaughan, James Taylor, Sade, Kenny Loggins, Basia, Little Feat, ZZ Top, and Tony Bennett, to name just a few. In addition, I've thrilled to the traveling Broadway shows *The Lion King*, *Cats*, *Wicked*, *Annie*, *Twelve Angry Men*, *Beauty and the Beast*, *On Your Feet!*, and *Beautiful* at the Majestic. Some of the movie *Selena* with Jennifer Lopez was filmed here. Yes, performing artists draw patrons into this 2,300-seat theater, but the venue itself is another draw. The 1929 Mediterranean-style theatre designed by John Eberson is an over-the-top Baroque fantasy that's listed on the National Register of Historic Places and is a National Historic Landmark. I get a charge every time I walk through the Majestic's doors. I never tire of checking out the fish in the aquarium, people-watching in the multi-level atrium, and gazing up at the ceiling's twinkling stars. If you haven't been to the Majestic or haven't been in awhile, what are you waiting on?

224 E. Houston St.
(210) 226-5700
majesticempire.com

GET YOUR CUMBIA GROOVE ON
WITH BOMBASTA BARRIO BIG BAND

San Antonio has its share of first-rate live bands, but if you have to pick just one to experience before you die, you must choose Bombasta Barrio Big Band. I first heard Robert Livar and his eight bandmates at PACfest, Palo Alto College's official Fiesta event. I was blown away by their fusion of cumbia, hip hop, funk, rock, and Latin jazz. Since then, I've seen them perform at various locations around town, including the Pearl's River Walk amphitheater. They never disappoint. Follow Bombasta on Facebook or Twitter or both so you don't miss a single performance. Hearing their music will lift your soul and transform avowed non-dancers into hip-shaking hoofers. Shakira will have nothing on you.

youtu.be/9923Ei6gjAU
bombasta.com

EXPERIENCE
THE MAGIC OF LIVE MUSIC

The live music scene in San Antonio is strong. In addition to catching major touring acts at the Tobin Center, the AT&T Center, the Alamodome, the Majestic, the Empire, and the Aztec, you can also get up close and personal with top-notch musicians at smaller venues here in the Alamo City. If you have to pick just five of the live music venues in the region, you can't go wrong with the following:

The Cove
thecove.us

Floore's Country Store
liveatfloores.com

Gruene Hall
gruenehall.com

Sam's Burger Joint
samsburgerjoint.com

The St. Mary's Strip (Paper Tiger, Limelight, Tycoon Flats, Hi-Tones, the Mix, the Phantom Room, Amp Room, Faust Tavern, the Squeezebox, Joey's, and La Botánica) on North St. Mary's Street, between 281 and East Dewey Place
stmarysstrip.com/places/#nightlife

ATTEND
ONE OF SAN ANTONIO'S
LIFE-AFFIRMING FESTIVALS

Music. Food. Dancing. *fun!* We're San Antonio, and you're invited to celebrate the fabulousness that is the Alamo City all year round.

Asian Festival: texancultures.com

Balcones Heights Jazz Festival: facebook.com/balconesheightsjazzfestival

Barbacoa & Big Red Festival: facebook.com/barbacoabigredfestival

Celebrate San Antonio: facebook.com/events/957541117773258

Chalk It Up: artpace.org/chalk-it-up

Cinco de Mayo: facebook.com/marketsquaresa

CineFestival: guadalupeculturalarts.org/cinefestival

Culinaria: culinariasa.org

Día de los Muertos: sacalaveras.com/category/events

Diez y Seis: facebook.com/marketsquaresa

Diwali Festival of Lights: diwalisa.com

Fiesta: fiesta-sa.org

Fotoseptiembre: fotoseptiembreusa.com

Fourth of July Celebration:
sanantonio.gov/ParksAndRec/News-Events/Events

Gospel and Soul Food Festival:
facebook.com/soul-food-festival-76856387237

Irish Festival: harpandshamrock.org/stpats.php

Jazz'SAlive: saparksfoundation.org/event/jazz-sa-live

Jewish Film Festival: jccsanantonio.org/filmfestival

Luminaria: luminariasa.org

Mariachi Vargas Extravaganza: mariachimusic.com

Oktoberfest: facebook.com/the.beethoven

Pride Festival: pridesanantonio.org/lgbtq-festival.html

Puerto Rican Heritage Festival: sociedadherenciaprsa.org

River City Rockfest: rivercityrockfest.com

San Antonio Book Festival: saplf.org/festival

San Antonio Film Festival: safilm.com

San Antonio Folk Dance Festival: safdf.org

Summer Art and Jazz Festival: sanantoniosummerartjazzfestival.com

Tejano Conjunto Festival: guadalupeculturalarts.org/tejano-conjunto-festival

Texas Folklife Festival: texancultures.com

Texas Salsa Festival: texassalsafest.com

World Heritage Festival: worldheritagefestival.org

DANCE THE NIGHT AWAY

San Antonio's dance club scene is rich with possibilities: techno, house, hip hop, country, new wave, industrial, salsa, bachata, merengue, and more. The three clubs you should not miss, however, were chosen with variety in mind. The Bonham Exchange in downtown San Antonio, a stone's throw from the Alamo, is a progressive, gay-friendly establishment that opened in 1981. Its 1892 building is alone worth the price of admission. Cowboys Dancehall on the city's Northeast Side is a cavernous place that reminds visitors that everything is bigger in Texas. For those who want to get their urban cowboy and cowgirl on, this is the place for you. Luna is a small, intimate venue with a Rat Pack vibe. Salsa, soul, R&B, Latin fusion, rockabilly, and more round out its live music scene. The music, tasty bar snacks, and affordable house cocktails make this North Side establishment a winner.

Bonham Exchange
bonhamexchange.com

Cowboys Dancehall
cowboysdancehall.com

Luna
lunalive.com

ESCAPE INTO AN ALTERNATE UNIVERSE
AT ONE OF SAN ANTONIO'S THEATERS

Drama. Comedy. Musicals. Tragedy. Improvisation. The Alamo City has it all. When the lights are dimmed and the curtain goes up, local playwrights, directors, actors, and techies pour their hearts and souls into revealing life's truths to the gathered audience. Notable San Antonio theaters include AtticRep, the Classic Theatre, Harlequin Dinner Theatre, Jump-Start Performance Co., the Magik Theatre, the Overtime Theater, Sheldon Vexler Theatre, the Public Theater of San Antonio, and Woodlawn Theatre. In addition to these, local colleges and universities have their own theater departments. Treat yourself to a show!

satheatre.com

SPORTS AND RECREATION

UNLEASH YOUR RIPARIAN NATURE
ALONG THE SAN ANTONIO RIVER

The Mission Reach Ecosystem Restoration and Recreation Project makes me weep tears of joy. Completed in 2013, the River Walk now extends from downtown San Antonio to just below Loop 410, a nine-mile stretch that encompasses the four Spanish colonial missions of the South Side. Walking, cycling, and kayaking along these wetlands are now a reality. Springtime is phenomenal. Bluebonnets, the state flower of Texas, line the hike and bike trails. Native wildlife, such as blue-winged teals, green herons, and red-shouldered hawks, are present throughout the year, with 153 bird species now identified. Keep your eyes peeled for spiny lizards, too. The $358-million project was definitely taxpayer money well spent. For those who'd like to roll down the reach, bicycles are available for rental at the Blue Star Arts Complex. Kayaks can be rented in Espada Park from Mission Kayak. Confluence Park, a three-acre park just north of where the San Antonio River and San Pedro Creek converge, provides a hands-on outdoor classroom for visitors to learn about the importance of water, conservation, environmental science, and sustainability.

sanantonioriver.org/mission_reach/mission_reach.php
confluencepark.sariverfound.org

STRETCH YOUR LEGS
ALONG THE MUSEUM REACH OF THE RIVER WALK

When my sister, good friend, and I were in France back in 1990, we shared a bottle of wine with an elderly man, a World War II veteran, whose brother now lives in the United States. He became verklempt while talking to us in his broken English. "Eets just so beautiful!" he exclaimed, wiping a tear from his eye. That's exactly how I feel about the five-mile extension of the River Walk from downtown all the way to Hildebrand Avenue. The Museum Reach is another hankie-producing happy cry. Thank you, city and county leaders, for making it and the Mission Reach so! From downtown, start your stroll along the San Antonio River at the Tobin Center for the Performing Arts and head north to the Pearl. On the way, be sure to stop in at the San Antonio Museum of Art. The Witte Museum, Brackenridge Park, and the San Antonio Zoo are also along this stretch. Is San Antonio great or what?!

sanantonioriver.org/museum_reach/museum_reach.php

CREATE LIFELONG MEMORIES
AT AMERICA'S OLDEST CHILDREN'S AMUSEMENT PARK

Generation after generation of San Antonio's children have experienced fun times at Kiddie Park, which opened its gates in 1925. It features eight rides—carousel, Ferris wheel, planes, boats, trains, helicopters, and flying saucers—that will thrill the toddler to elementary school-aged set. Children can also enjoy pony rides on the weekends and ice skating during the winter months, along with arcade and carnival games throughout the year. Renovated in 2009, Kiddie Park is a happy place that's perfect for snapping treasured family photos. Snack on cotton candy, popcorn, or ice cream while you're there.

3015 Broadway
(210) 824-4351
kiddiepark.com

ESCAPE INTO NATURE
AT BRACKENRIDGE PARK

Brackenridge Park is yet another of San Antonio's rejuvenating urban oases. Minutes from the center of downtown, you will find yourself surrounded by tall trees and a less-traveled stretch of the San Antonio River. The 344-acre park underwent a major renovation not long ago, and three walking trails opened to the public: Waterworks (1.5 miles), Wildlife (1 mile), and Wildnerness (.75 miles). Public art is found along each trail, and inviting picnic tables dot the landscape. Don't miss Dionicio Rodriguez's 1926 *faux bois* ("false wood") footbridge. The San Antonio Zoo and its miniature train, the San Antonio Zoo Eagle, are also located in the park. However, when you need a place to clear your head and commune with some koi, head to the park's sunken gardens, officially named the San Antonio Japanese Tea Garden. You can make your visit a two-for-one (gardens/zoo), three-for-one (gardens/zoo/miniature train), or four-for-one (gardens/zoo/miniature train/park) adventure. Notice, however, that the gardens are a given. Don't miss them! Plus, you won't have to shell out any dinero. Admission to the gardens is free.

3700 N. St. Mary's
(210) 207-8480
sanantonio.gov/parksandrec

VISIT
ONE OF THE NATION'S OLDEST PARKS, SAN PEDRO SPRINGS

Stroll through San Pedro Springs Park, San Antonio's oldest park and the second-oldest park in the nation. (OK, Boston, so you bested us there, but I think our park is prettier than yours, so there!) According to historians, Native Americans gathered at San Pedro Springs and Creek more than twelve thousand years ago, and the Spaniards settled here in the late 1600s. Stunning cypress trees line the artistically designed pool that looks like it's spring fed, but it's not. Therefore, you won't freeze your you-know-whats off like you do at Barton Springs Pool in Austin. The real springs are visible just north of the pool, but you're not supposed to swim in them because of the potential damage you may cause. The pool is run by the City of San Antonio, and it is open during the summer months. Admission is free, but you do have to wear proper swimming attire to get in. During the rest of the year, enjoy a picnic at one of the many tables or benches. Check out the San Pedro Branch Library, too.

2200 N. Flores
(210) 732-5992
sanantonio.gov/parksandrec

SAY SÍ! (YES!)
TO FITNESS AT SÍCLOVÍA

Síclovía, San Antonio's spin on the Ciclovía in Bogotá, Colombia, started in October 2011, making two miles of Broadway car-free for folks to enjoy outdoor recreational sports and activities without having to worry about being run over. Skateboarders, walkers, runners, hula hoopers, skaters, tricyclers, bicyclers, bubble-blowers, strollers, scooters, and dog lovers look forward to this free twice-per-year event. Síclovía's slogan, "Go play in the street!," should add "and parks" in parentheses. The YMCA sets up stages along the route to give attendees a taste of Zumba, kickboxing, Pilates, and more. Down Broadway at Lions Field, hula hoops may be at the ready, along with giant chess boards and bubble wands. A taekwondo presentation might demonstrate this South Korean martial art. Some years, you can even Zumba in front of the Alamo! Kick-start your path to fitness at this fun, family-friendly, bi-annual event.

ymcasatx.org/siclovia

PLAY THE "WORLD'S FINEST"
MINIATURE GOLF COURSE, COOL CREST

Cool Crest Miniature Golf claims to be the world's finest, and who's to argue with them? Set atop the apex of Fredericksburg Road within sight of Interstate 10, this tropical paradise has been a San Antonio recreational staple since 1929. Two eighteen-hole courses are challenging, yet fun. I had a pretty good run until I got to hole thirteen, not so lucky, and hole fourteen, which ran uphill. Despite these two setbacks, my overall score was decent. As the encouraging lady at the front desk said when I returned my putter, "Practice makes perfect!" Harold and Maria Metzger ran Cool Crest for almost seventy years. In 2013, the Andry family took over, and they've continued in the Metzgers' footsteps. Why mess with the world's finest?! The beautiful landscaping draws a variety of butterflies and is a welcome antidote to screen-time overload. And don't forget to stop by El Paraiso Ice Cream after you've played. (Take a right from the Cool Crest parking lot onto Fredericksburg.) Losers have to treat winners to a paleta!

1402 Fredericksburg Rd.
(210) 732-0222
coolcrestgolf.com

PAINT YOUR FACE FOR COLLEGE BALL

The Valero Alamo Bowl has been providing zealous fans a college football fix since 1993. The second-choice team of the Pac-12 Conference goes up against the third-choice team of the Big 12 Conference in late December or early January at the downtown Alamodome, which seats 65,000. Over the years, UCLA kicked Kansas State; TCU beat Stanford; Oklahoma State bested Colorado; and Baylor triumphed over Washington. More than one thousand high school musicians, dancers, and cheerleaders wow at the halftime show. To take advantage of the Alamo Bowl's holiday time period, the event's organizers prepare a Bowl Week Itinerary to maximize your stay in the Alamo City. Check out the website. Whether your team is in the game or not, a good time is guaranteed.

100 Montana St.
(210) 226-2695
alamobowl.com

TAKE IN A SPURS GAME
AT THE AT&T CENTER

When a friend of mine was in Madrid, Spain, he and his family wandered into a prohibited military area in the center of the city. Before they realized their mistake, the Guardia Civil, the city's police force, surrounded them. My friend, a former Marine who speaks Spanish, raised his hands over his head and said, "Lo siento. No somos de aquí. Somos de San Antonio, Texas." (We're sorry. We're not from here. We're from San Antonio, Texas.) One of the guards smiled and replied, "Los Spurs!" Yes, the San Antonio Spurs have put the Alamo City on the world's map. With an international set of players along with those from the United States, the National Basketball Association champions make San Antonio proud. Coach Gregg "Pop" Popovich has brought out the best in the team since 1996. The players are known for being gentlemen both on and off the court. From the end of October through April, don't miss your opportunity to witness greatness in action. ¡Viva los Spurs!

1 AT&T Center Parkway
(210) 444-5000
nba.com/spurs/tickets

GET YOUR FILL
OF BRONC RIDERS AND BARREL RACERS AT THE STOCK SHOW & RODEO

If it's February, it must be the rodeo! Trail riders from across the state make their way to this Texas-sized event, rain or shine. The San Antonio Stock Show & Rodeo is one of the country's largest, with attendance that tops 1.5 million. More than six thousand volunteers make it happen. Every year since 2005, it's won the Professional Rodeo Cowboys Association's Large Rodeo of the Year Award. Over a three-week period, attendees enjoy bronc and bull riders, barrel racers, and mutton busters, along with top-rate entertainment, such as Willie Nelson, Reba McEntire, and Keith Urban. More than $160 million has been given to the youth of Texas via scholarships, grants, calf scrambles, and show premiums since 1984. In the livestock barns, visitors can commune with beef cattle, dairy cattle, chickens, turkeys, goats, pigs, and sheep. Visitors will also enjoy an on-site carnival, pony rides, a petting zoo, and a swine sprint. Shopping and food round out the event. If you've never had a bucking bull almost land in your lap, you haven't lived.

723 AT&T Center Parkway
(210) 225-5851
sarodeo.com

LET YOUR SPIRIT SOAR
AT MORGAN'S WONDERLAND

Morgan's Wonderland is the world's first theme park designed for individuals with special needs. The Hartman family created the park so that people with and without disabilities could come together to have fun and learn how to better understand one another. The $36-million outdoor park features rides, playgrounds, gardens, a catch-and-release fishing lake, a miniature train, an amphitheater, and picnic areas that are all wheelchair accessible. The twenty-five-acre park opened in 2010, and it has already hosted more than one million guests from all fifty states and sixty-nine countries. Its $17-million ultra splash park, Morgan's Inspiration Island, opened in 2017. Entry into Morgan's Wonderland is a bargain, and parking is free! You can purchase your tickets online.

5223 David Edwards Dr.
(210) 495-5888
morganswonderland.com

RUN 26.2 OR 13.1 OR 6.2 OR 3.1 MILES
AT THE ROCK 'N' ROLL MARATHON

More than thirty Rock 'n' Roll Marathons are held around the world, but San Antonio's is the only one that has the Alamo on its route. Trinity University, King William, Mission San Jose, and the Mission Reach portion of the River Walk are also included. Live bands, cheerleaders, and an army of volunteers give the thirty thousand participants the lift they need to make it across the finish line and into the party and headliner concert at the Alamodome. Not a runner? No problem! You can also walk. Dancing is optional.

runrocknroll.com/san-antonio

COMMUNE WITH NATURE
IN SAN ANTONIO'S NATURAL AREAS

In addition to San Antonio's city parks, the Alamo City is fortunate to have eight natural areas or preserves within its city limits: Crownridge Canyon, Eisenhower Park, Friedrich Wilderness Park, Government Canyon, Phil Hardberger Park, Medina River, Panther Springs, and Walker Ranch Historic Landmark Park. Crownridge's 207 acres, part of the Edwards Aquifer Protection Program, offer hillside vistas and forested canyon bottoms. Friedrich, home of the endangered golden-cheeked warbler, offers 5.5 miles of hiking. Government Canyon, a state natural area "where the Texas Hill Country begins," is located on more than 7,500 acres of the aquifer's recharge zone and has more than forty miles of trails. The South Side's Medina River Natural Area is a 511-acre preserve along the banks of what was once the official boundary between Texas and Mexico. Phil Hardberger covers more than three hundred acres on the city's North Side and boasts one of the best dog parks in town. And don't forget the internationally known Mitchell Lake Audubon Center, a 1,200-acre natural area on the South Side.

sanantonio.gov/ParksAndRec/ParksFacilities/AllParksFacilities/
A-ZParksFacilitiesIndex.aspx
tpwd.texas.gov/state-parks/government-canyon
sanaturalareas.org
mitchelllake.audubon.org

RELEASE YOUR INNER CHILD
AT YANAGUANA GARDEN

Hemisfair, the site of the 1968 World's Fair that celebrated San Antonio's 250th birthday, is undergoing a $30-million renovation to turn itself into a world-class urban park in downtown San Antonio. Yanaguana Garden, an outdoor play area for both children and adults, is the first area of the park to re-open. Nestled along César Chávez Boulevard and South Alamo Street, the four-acre park features a Parque Güell-like giant blue panther covered in mosaic tiles and glass beads by local artist Oscar Alvarado. The *PanterAzul* begs to be climbed and photographed. Seven additional local artists joined in creating this engaging space that includes a giant sandbox, a splash pad, climbing structures, a performance-ready stage, and more. Hemisfair is open seven days a week from 7 a.m. until midnight.

434 S. Alamo St.
(210) 709-4750
hemisfair.org

LEARN HOW TO WALK LIKE A PENGUIN
AT SEAWORLD SAN ANTONIO

SeaWorld of San Antonio gives visitors a chance to get up close and personal with sea life, including penguins in their frosty habitat. If penguins aren't your thing, dolphins, sea lions, alligators, flamingos, belugas, and more are at the ready. Seven big-production shows and five spine-tingling rides, including the Great White and Steel Eel, will keep you hopping. If that's not enough, you may want to purchase an add-on Aquatica water park ticket. Restaurants and concession stands are located throughout the park, but you might want to consider packing a lunch to eat outside the entrance. You might also consider taking the #64 VIA bus to avoid the $20 parking fee. SeaWorld is big, so be sure to wear comfortable shoes.

10500 SeaWorld Dr.
(210) 520-4732
seaworldparks.com/seaworld-sanantonio

HOLD ON TIGHT
AT SIX FLAGS FIESTA TEXAS

Six Flags Fiesta Texas is known for its nine scream-inducing roller coasters: Batman, Boomerang, Fireball, Goliath, Iron Rattler, Pandemonium, Poltergeist, Road Runner, and Superman: Krypton Coaster. (And more are on the way!) For those who are roller coaster averse, the two-hundred-acre park also offers forty other rides, live entertainment, food, shopping, and a water park with a Texas-shaped wave pool. Six Flags Fiesta Texas stages various events throughout the year, such as Spring Break, Fourth of July, Halloween, and the holidays, to name a few. To save some money, buy your tickets and parking online. VIA's #94 Fiesta Texas Express runs from downtown. All ages, from grandkids to grandparents, will enjoy this family-friendly park that is located in a former rock quarry.

17000 IH-10 West
(210) 697-5050
sixflags.com/fiestatexas

VISIT
TEXAS'S LARGEST UNDERGROUND CAVERNS

The odds of most of us traveling into space are pretty slim. However, traveling into the Earth is within our reach. Just thirty minutes from the Alamo, Natural Bridge Caverns gives explorers a chance to venture 180 feet below ground and finally learn the difference between stalactites and stalagmites on this seventy-five-minute walking tour. Ancient formations, including flowstones, chandeliers, totem poles, fried eggs, soda straws, and the sixty-foot limestone slab bridge, will inspire awe. Wear rubber-soled shoes with good tread, as the pathways can be slippery. Strollers are not recommended.

26495 Natural Bridge Caverns Rd.
(210) 651-6101
naturalbridgecaverns.com

SHOPPING AND FASHION

SEARCH FOR A PERFECT GIFT
AT FIESTA ON MAIN

When the grandmother of my childhood friend would bemoan an unsuccessful shopping trip, she'd sniff, "I didn't even open my purse." This will not be your problem at Fiesta on Main, a store whose motto, "Where Mexico is closer than you think, and Fiesta never ends!," is an understatement. Fiesta on Main specializes in folk art, talavera pottery, Fiesta decorations, piñatas, paper flowers, flower garland crowns, papel picado, confetti eggs, furniture, wedding decorations, Day of the Dead items, Christmas decorations, clothing, and more. "And more" does not begin to address its inventory. Fiesta on Main is not for minimalists. Every square inch of space is crammed with something wonderful that you will want to bring home with you or give to a friend. My maternal grandmother's maxim comes to mind: "Don't buy anything you need, darlin'. Just buy something you want." You'll find plenty you want at Fiesta on Main, and, for out-of-town guests, one-stop souvenir shopping has never been easier.

2025 N. Main Ave.
(210) 738-1188

102 W. Rector
(210) 801-9900

alamofiesta.com

FEED YOUR CREATIVITY
AT LAS COLCHAS

If you want to lower your blood pressure and recharge your creative batteries, Las Colchas is the place for you. Even if you've never handled a needle and thread in your life, you'll be welcomed and inspired by this quaint quilt shop tucked away in downtown San Antonio. It's always a joy just to walk in to see what's on display. Plus, the owners, Francine and Toni, always have coffee and treats set out for their guests. What's not to like about that?! Las Colchas has fabric to suit every taste: traditional, Tex-Mex (including fabrics for El Día de Los Muertos), modern (Kaffe Fassett), international, and more. Plus, it has ready-made kits for those who don't have a clue how to get started. I've taken four classes at Las Colchas: crazy quilt, vintage embroidery, prayer flags, and punched embroidery. From each class, I walked away with a handmade treasure to enjoy now before passing it on to the next generation. What will you make?

110 Ogden St.
(210) 223-2405
lascolchas.com

CHECK OUT
THE WORLD'S LARGEST COWBOY BOOTS AT NORTH STAR MALL

San Antonio, like every large city, has its share of shopping destinations, but North Star Mall is one of the city's best places to part with your hard-earned cash, and it's the only place that has a giant pair of cowboy boots set out to welcome you. North Star, which is on NW Loop 410 between the San Pedro and McCullough exits, turned fifty in 2010, and it has aged well. Anchored by Macy's, Dillard's, Saks Fifth Avenue, JCPenney, and Forever 21, North Star Mall has about two hundred tenants. H&M, Abercrombie & Fitch, Michael Kors, Kate Spade, the Disney Store, Build-A-Bear Workshop, Gap, Talbots, Victoria's Secret, Armani Exchange, Fossil, Guess, Steve Madden, Apple, Microsoft, Dallas Cowboys Pro Shop, Godiva Chocolatier, and more offer something to suit every age and disposition. The distance between San Pedro and McCullough is about half a mile, so you'll log a mile if you walk from one end to the other and back, and that doesn't include detours along the way. Happy shopping! If North Star Mall doesn't quench your shopping thirst, try the Shops at La Cantera, located off Loop 1604 near Six Flags Fiesta Texas.

7400 San Pedro Ave.
(210) 340-6627
northstarmall.com

STEP YOUR WAY TO GOOD HEALTH
AT THE PEARL

Just when you think that ten thousand steps a day is enough to help stave off diabetes and heart disease, it turns out that fifteen thousand steps is what we actually need to maintain a normal body mass index and metabolic profile. Instead of enduring a ho-hum treadmill to get your steps in, stroll down the Museum Reach of the River Walk from downtown and enjoy shopping your way across the Pearl. Adelante Boutique, Bike World, Curio at Hotel Emma, Dos Carolinas, Lawrence Markey, LeeLee Shoes, Leighelena, Niche Boutique, the Sporting District, Ten Thousand Villages, the Tiny Finch, the Twig Book Shop (where you can pick up extra copies of this book!), and the Vintage Bouquet Bar will scratch every shopping itch you have.

Pearl Parkway at Broadway
atpearl.com/goods-services

UNEARTH A TREASURE OR TWO
AT SAN ANTONIO'S BEST VINTAGE/ THRIFT/RESALE STORES

One of my favorite things to do when I'm traveling outside of San Antonio is to visit local vintage/thrift/resale shops. You never know what to-die-for items you're going to encounter while you're on your treasure hunt. Plus, thrift store finds make much better souvenirs than ho-hum refrigerator magnets, T-shirts, and shot glasses. Two vintage Paris streetscapes that I purchased in Michigan while on a massive cross-country road trip hang on my bedroom wall. San Antonio has heaps of treasure-laden vintage, thrift, and consignment/resale stores. I've always thought we'd make a great location for HGTV's *Flea Market Flip*. (How 'bout it, Lara?!) Let the hunt begin!

Alamo Antique Mall
125 Broadway St.
facebook.com/alamoantiquemall

Antiques at Broadway
5226 Broadway St.
facebook.com/antiquesatbroadwaysanantonio

Assistance League Thrift House
2611 West Ave.
assistanceleague.org/san-antonio/thrift-shop

Boysville Thrift Store
307 W. Olmos Dr.
boysvillethriftstore.com

Green Door Thrift Shop
1030 Nacogdoches Rd.
slecsa.org/the-green-door

Off My Rocker
204 W. Olmos Dr.
yoursiteguy.com/offmyrockerindex.html

Shops at Blanco Roundabout
(The Junction, Karolina's, San Antonio Furniture Finders,
House of History, Re-Creations by Rita, Graced Gifts,
and the Marcantile)
Blanco Road at Fulton Avenue
facebook.com/shopsatblanco

Yeyas Antiques & Oddities
1423 E. Commerce St.
yeyasantiques.net

BEAT SANTA TO THE PUNCH
AT THE ESPERANZA PEACE MARKET

The Esperanza Peace and Justice Center's annual Mercado de Paz is open only the two days after Thanksgiving each year. Don't miss it! You never know what or whom you're going to run across when you're at the market. One year, it was with great pleasure and awe that I encountered Irene Aguilar Alcántara, one of the famed Aguilar sisters, ceramic artists extraordinaire from Oaxaca, Mexico, right here in our very own San Antonio. My husband and I had toured the Aguilar sisters' studios in Mexico, but there's only so much you can bring back on the plane. It was a real joy to be able to chat with Irene and buy *Frida Muerta*, a piece of her folk art, for a mere $20. Not all of the artists at the Mercado de Paz are from out of town. Many home-grown artists are also present. I spied an oh-so-wonderful brightly colored crocheted toque and *had* to have it, especially when I found out that it cost only $8. As I walked through the market, several people said how much they loved my chapeau. In other words, insta-compliments. See what you'll find at the market, San Antonio's remedy for Black Friday!

922 San Pedro Ave.
(210) 228-0201
esperanzacenter.org

BROWSE TO YOUR HEART'S CONTENT
AT THE FLEA MART

You never know what you're going to find at a flea market, and that's half the fun. The other half is a combination of people watching, corn-on-the-cob eating, and conjunto dancing. Although the San Antonio region has more than a dozen flea markets, I suggest you head south to the Flea Mart on the Poteet Highway, just outside of Loop 410. There you will find an enormous selection of piñatas, personalized T-shirts, quinceañera gowns, religious holy cards, Our Lady of Guadalupe key chains, and leather cowboy boots made in Guanajuato, Mexico. You can even purchase your own grave marker at the Flea Mart. Ice-cold beer, raspas (snow cones), and cotton candy make strolling around this paved and covered flea market even nicer. The Flea Mart is open every Saturday and Sunday from 10 a.m. to 6 p.m. Parking costs $2, but it's free before 10 a.m. Live conjunto music starts at noon both days.

12280 Poteet Jourdanton Freeway (Hwy. 16)
(210) 624-2666
fleamarketsanantonio.com

HUNT FOR GARDEN FAIRIES
AT SHADES OF GREEN

One of my friends goes to Shades of Green whenever she's feeling blue. "You just can't be sad there," she said. I have to agree. Shades of Green will put anyone in a good mood. Meandering pathways, soothing fountains, cedar arbors, and blooming flowers are sure to lift your spirits. It's a gardener's dream. Even if you're not a gardener, you'll want to become one. It's that inspiring. The knowledgeable, friendly staff at Shades of Green will teach you about native plants and the benefits of organic gardening while you're there, but if you'd like to learn more, free Saturday seminars begin at 9:45 a.m. The coffee is on at 9 a.m. Looking for a perfect gift for your gardening friends and family? Shades of Green will have it. Be sure to put this neighborhood nursery on your feel-good list!

334 W. Sunset Rd.
(210) 824-3772
shadesofgreensa.com

SUGGESTED
ITINERARIES

ARTS AND CULTURE

Artpace, 7

Blue Star Contemporary Art Museum, 7, 84

Briscoe Western Art Museum, 7

Carver Community Cultural Center, 42

Guadalupe Cultural Arts Center, 45

McNay Art Museum, 6–7

San Antonio Museum of Art, 7, 101

Texas Folklife Festival, 5, 95

Tobin Center for the Performing Arts, 90

Witte Museum, 26, 101

TOP TEN

Because San Antonio is filled with so much fabulousness, it's difficult to choose just ten. (That's why I cheated a little on the double/triple entries below. *Perdóname.* Think of them as either/or options, even though I recommend *all* of them.)

The Alamo, 2

Breakfast tacos, 58

Christmas lights on the River Walk, 90

Japanese Tea Garden/Brackenridge Park/San Antonio Zoo, 24, 103

McNay Art Museum/San Antonio Museum of Art, 6–7

Mission Reach, 14, 100

San Antonio Botanical Garden, 22

San Fernando Cathedral, 18

TOP TEN FREE THINGS TO DO

FUN WITH KIDS

PURO SAN ANTONIO

LONG WEEKEND GETAWAY

Arrive Thursday evening

Friday schedule

Saturday schedule

Japanese Tea Garden (also known as Sunken Gardens), 103

San Antonio Zoo, 24

Dinner at Augie's Barbed Wire Smokehouse or Demo's Greek Food, 61, 70

Drinks at Hotel Emma's Sternewirth Tavern, 77

Sunday schedule

Mass at San Fernando Cathedral, 18

Breakfast tacos at Panchito's, Taco Garage, El Milagrito, or Pete's Tako House, 58–59

McNay Art Museum (opens at noon on Sunday), 6–7

Depart Sunday afternoon

HISTORY BUFF

The Alamo, 2

Casa Navarro State Historic Site, 25

Fort Sam Houston Museum, 33

Institute of Texan Cultures, 5

Mission Reach, 14, 100

San Fernando Cathedral, 18

San Fernando Cemetery Number Two/East Side cemeteries, 16, 47

Spanish Governor's Palace, 38

Spirit Reach (headwaters of the San Antonio River), 52

Villa Finale/Steves Homestead, 12

DOWNTOWN

The Alamo, 2

Bexar County Courthouse, 51

La Villita/Arneson River Theatre, 11

El Mercado, 37

NORTH

SOUTH

ACTIVITIES
BY SEASON

SPRING

SUMMER

FALL

WINTER

INDEX